PETER FRITZSCHE

My
Hamster

BARRON'S

CONTENTS

Welcome Home

Good Food for Health and Fitness

5 Well-cared For and Totally Healthy

6 Activity and Wellness

When Hamsters Have Babies

What to Do When There Are Problems

Appendix

The Typical Hamster

Although hamsters are definitely night owls,
they are among the most popular pets. Hardly anyone
can resist their adorable looks and droll ways.

The Story of the Golden Hamster

The first golden hamsters appeared in Europe around 75 years ago as the offspring of a pair of siblings. From then on their millionfold distribution as pets was only a matter of time, given their enormous fertility.

Golden hamsters, also known as Syrian hamsters, are indubitably cute animals. Seen in a picture or "live" in a pet store, they are nearly irresistible, with their button eyes and their droll ways. Probably for this reason, hamster breeders do not have to complain about decreasing sales.

But I probably should not have written this book at all, for hamsters—at least golden hamsters—are not particularly suited for everyone. The reasons are clear:

▶ Golden hamsters are not very sociable (see page 17).
▶ They only become active when humans want to sleep.
▶ Their life expectancy is quite short, at about two years.
▶ They are easily stressed.

Therefore, before you buy one, consider very carefully whether a hamster is actually suitable for your idea of pet keeping and for your home. If you then try conscientiously to meet the animal's life needs, you have the best prospect of providing this funny little pet with the most appropriate maintenance possible. And this should be the goal of every hamster keeper. We have only quite recently begun to investigate the biolo-gy of hamsters living in the wild. The findings offer an excellent foundation for providing optimal living conditions for the hamster kept as a pet.

Some Necessary Taxonomy

All animals and plants have a scientific name, which is most often of Latin or Greek origin. The marvelous thing about it is that this name is unique, and any animal lover anywhere in the world who knows an animal's scientific name will be able to communicate with others. The scientific name always consists of two parts: the genus, for example,

From the wild form of the golden hamster, numerous breeds have been developed, like this variant with a lighter fur color. ▶

Cricetus (hamster) or *Mesocricetus* (*meso* = middle, so middle hamster), and the species, for example, *aurantus* (golden). Within the animal kingdom the hamster belongs to the phylum of the chordates (Chordata; the chord is a supporting "rod" that in higher animals becomes the spinal column) and to the class of mammals (Mammalia). Among the mammals, hamsters are in the order that has the greatest number of species, the rodents (Rodentia). The rodents consist of four suborders. Hamsters are close to mice and therefore are classified with the mouse relatives (Myomorpha). The next lower category is the family of the burrowers (Cricetidae). The true hamsters form a subfamily (Cricetinae) with a few other animals. The nine hamster genera belong to these, with *Mesocricetus* being one, *Phodopus* another. In this guide, five species are described:

▸ Syrian golden hamster (*Mesocricetus auratus),*
▸ Djungarian dwarf hamster (*Phodopus sungorus),*
▸ Campbell's dwarf hamster (*Phodopus campbelli),*
▸ Roborovski dwarf hamster (*Phodopus roborovskii),* and
▸ Chinese striped hamster (*Cricetulus griseus).*

1 **Cautiously** a golden hamster emerges from his burrow in a field of lentils in southern Turkey. The plastic ring around the opening is furnished with antennae and photoelectric beams, which permit monitoring of the activity.

2 **Golden hamster** in its natural habitat leaving its burrow after sunrise. The insecure hamster creeps, pressed against the ground, into the safety of the plant cover.

The field hamster lives in Europe. It is the largest of the hamster species. ▶

The Discovery of the Golden Hamster

When "hamsters" are mentioned, almost everyone first thinks of the Syrian golden hamster. But there are still more than 20 other hamster species. One, the field hamster, is native to Europe, and at least four other species are kept as pets (see pages 25–29). The golden hamster was first mentioned in the literature in 1797, but it was not described scientifically until 1839. George Robert Waterhouse described it on the basis of a prepared specimen (a dead animal) from the British Museum in London. It received the scientific name *Mesocricetus auratus*, which can be translated as "golden middle hamster." However, almost 100 years passed before living golden hamsters were found and could start their triumphant progress into the world.

On April 12, 1930, for the first time, workers digging under the direction of the Israeli Professor Aharoni dug out a mother with eleven young in an Arab wheat field in the vicinity of the Syrian city of Aleppo. Of these animals, some were killed for scientific investigation; others escaped from their cage with wooden flooring and drowned in a swimming pool. In the end, there remained only one female and three males. All the golden hamsters kept as pets in the entire world come from this mating of brothers and sister! By the end of the first year, the animals already had 150 offspring.

In 1931, golden hamsters were brought to France and England; in 1938, to the United States; and in 1948, after the Second World War, to Germany. Thanks to their winsome appearance and their ability to reproduce easily, they enjoyed great popularity everywhere, and soon they were for sale in many pet stores.

Expedition into golden hamster land

For a long time, nothing was known about golden hamsters living in the wild, and they were even thought to be extinct. Professor Gattermann and his colleagues undertook an expedition into the Syrian high plains in 1999. I also took part in this expedition. With advice from Syrian farmers, we were able to dig out living golden hamsters, bring 19 animals back to Halle,

Germany, and successfully breed them. Today the number of golden hamsters living in the wild is estimated to be about 100,000. Against that, one assumes that seven million to eight million golden hamsters are living in cages as pets, which are all the offspring of the single brother-sister mating of 1930 (see page 9). This of course means that

The Habitat of Wild Hamsters

All hamster species are found only in Europe and Asia in the northern hemisphere. Their distribution ranges from France in the west to China in the east. **Golden hamsters:** The range of the Syrian golden hamster is bounded by natural barriers (mountains and water bodies) in the north of Syria and the extreme south of Turkey. Originally the

DID YOU KNOW THAT...

. . . at one time, field hamsters were greatly hunted?

The field hamster, native to Europe, used to be considered a pest, since it was found in every wheat field and had carried large quantities of grains into its burrow. In some burrows up to 23 pounds (50 kg) of wheat were found! Hamster trappers were paid a cash bounty per number of captured animals. Today there are only a few field hamsters left, and there are extensive protective measures in place so that they do not disappear from our environment entirely.

later inbreeding has practically always occurred among the descendents of that mating. Genetic research shows a relatively uniform profile of genetic information among the pets, in comparison to really large differences among their fellow species members in the wild. On the other hand, scientists themselves were amazed that there were only a few external differences between pet or laboratory golden hamsters and wild ones. Precise measurements of activity usually did show differences (see page 18).

golden hamster lived in the steppe regions, but today it is chiefly found in fields. Golden hamsters appear to prefer burrows in fields in which lentils or chick peas are grown. In its native habitat, the golden hamster is subject to very extreme temperature fluctuations. Sometimes the temperature in summer will sink from over 86°F (30°C) in the daytime down to 41°F (5°C) at night. There will be frost about thirty days during the winter, and temperatures can sink to 16°F (–9°C). In addition, drought predominates in summer, with practically no rainfall from July to

The little golden hamster transports up to
0.7 ounces (20 grams) of wheat kernels in its
cheek pouches to fill up its feed stores in the burrow.

September. So the golden hamster spends most of its life in its underground burrow, which it has filled with food reserves during the good times.

Dwarf or short-tailed hamster: We will continue to use the term *dwarf hamsters* in this guide, since this has become the established name for the little fellows. Scientifically, however, these animals are termed *short-tailed hamsters*. When you know furthermore that this animal is called *desert hamster* in America, you understand more clearly that it is very useful to know the scientific name of your hamster.

Dwarf hamsters can be found in the steppes (or plains), deserts, and semideserts of Russia, Mongolia, and China. Djungarian dwarf hamsters are found farthest west. To some extent, their habitat overlaps that of the field hamster described below. They prefer grass plains.

Roborovski dwarf hamsters and Campbell's dwarf hamsters, on the other hand, are found only farther to the east, spreading almost to China. Both species live more in sandy, partly desertlike areas. The Chinese striped hamster is found the farthest east; its range is from China to the Pacific Ocean.

Dwarf hamsters are found in deserts and semideserts in Russia, Mongolia, and China.

Field hamsters: A wild hamster species, which also can be found in Germany and which is not suitable as a pet, the field hamster (*Cricetus cricetus*) is the largest and the most widely distributed hamster. It is under protection in Germany.

Wildlife conservation groups as well as governments are engaged in protecting the field hamster. In Europe, field hamsters are found as far west as the Netherlands, where only very few are still living. They are also very strongly protected there. Farmers even receive money from the government to keep their fields "hamster-friendly." In the east, one can find field hamsters as far as the Yenisei River in central Siberia.

Very rarely does a golden hamster happen on such a colossal find in the wild.
▼

Size and Weight of the Hamster

Size: Golden hamsters grow to be about 7 in. (18 cm) long. The dwarf hamster (short-tailed hamster) remains small. Thus the Chinese dwarf hamster becomes up to 5 in. (13 cm) in size, while Campbell's and Djungarian dwarf hamsters only grow up to 3.9 in. (10 cm) long.

The smallest of the entire hamster species discussed here is the Roborovski dwarf hamster with a length of up to 1.5 in. (4–5 cm).

Weight: The golden hamster can weigh up to 6.4 ounces (180 g); the females are frequently heavier than the males. Dwarf hamsters are lightweights at a maximum of 1.76 ounces (50 g).

Golden hamsters love to climb and have no problem overcoming obstacles. You should always offer your pet hamster natural materials for climbing.

How Hamsters Live

For the correct maintenance of the hamster, it is important not only to know its physical requirements but also to be knowledgable about its sensory capabilities, habits, and behavior.

One can hardly confuse golden hamsters because of their looks and their size. Dwarf hamsters, on the other hand, are sometimes difficult to tell apart.

Differentiating Among Dwarf Hamsters

Roborovski dwarf hamster: Unlike the other three species, the Roborovski dwarf hamster has no black stripe down its back. It is also somewhat smaller.
Chinese dwarf hamster: It is somewhat more striped and looks more mouselike than the more compact *Phodopus* dwarf hamsters. Besides, it has a longer tail than the other dwarf hamsters. The tail extends beyond its hind feet.
Djungarian and Campbell's dwarf hamsters: It is more difficult not to confuse the remaining species. At first sight, the Djungarian and Campbell's dwarf hamsters appear very similar, so much so that they used to be considered one species. Both have a black stripe on the back and a relatively short tail. You can tell the difference by keeping your dwarf hamsters at natural temperatures. During the shortening days before winter, only the Djungarian dwarf hamster will begin to change

color: beginning with the belly side, it will slowly get a white winter coat. This is also the reason that, even in summer, there is a clear contrast between the white belly side and the gray-brown upper side. On the other hand, in winter the whitish coloration of the underside of the Campbell's dwarf hamster changes to the more yellowish brown coloration of the upper side. The line between upper and underside blurs and makes three arcs (accordingly also called the three arc line), which is more easily recognizable in the Djungarian dwarf hamsters. Besides, the back line in the Djungarian dwarf hamster is distinctly black, whereas it is more of a dark brown in the Campbell's dwarf hamster.

The Biology of the Hamster

Cheek pouches: Hamsters use their cheek pouches in the mucous membrane of the mouth as pockets. They reach almost to the rear legs and allow the hamster to move food into the burrow. To better hold the transported material, the cheek pouches are covered with rough skin and bristles, so that often the front legs must be used to help empty them. But normally the cheek pouches cannot be turned out from outside because they are held closed by a special muscle.

The internal structure of the golden hamster: It resembles the anatomy of all mammals. Unusual features are the two-chambered stomach (a first stomach for storing food and a glandular stomach for digestion), a relatively large blind gut (cecum), and in females, a two-chambered womb (uterus).

Teeth: Golden hamsters have four incisors and twelve molars. The incisors keep growing and therefore the hamster must always have an opportunity to wear them down.

Toes: The forelegs have four toes visible; the fifth has receded. The back legs, on the other hand, clearly have five toes.

Skeleton: The skeleton of the hamster is quite fragile and brittle. Although hamsters possess a so-called cliff avoidance behavior (→ Feeling, page 16), they will jump down from great heights (e.g., from the edge of the table), especially if they feel cornered. But unlike other animals, cats, for instance, they cannot cushion the shocks of these jumps, so that broken bones are often the result.

Sexing: Differentiating between males and females is not easy. The most reliable characteristic difference is the distance between the sexual opening and the anus; it is generally greater in the male. In the summer months, in particular, the testicles of the male golden hamster emerge at higher temperatures. This is necessary for the development of the male hamster's sperm, which is formed in the testicles. The sperm cannot be exposed to high temperatures without affecting the animal's ability to reproduce.

The Sensory Capabilities

The sensory capabilities include seeing, hearing, smelling, and feeling. These senses are developed to different degrees in the hamster.

How well hamsters see

Golden hamsters have relatively large eyes, with which they can take in a broad visual field. On the other hand, their eyesight is quite poorly developed. Hamsters are generally considered short-sighted and can only make out shapes clearly at distances of about 40 in. (1 m). Experiments have shown that in comparison to, say, rats, hamsters take much longer to recognize different shapes. Their ability to see colors

◀ *Golden hamsters are loners. Never, ever keep two animals in one cage or it can lead to ferocious quarrels that may result in death.*

appears to be equally poor. In contrast to humans, hamsters are, like most land-living mammals, dichromates, which have only two cone types for color in the retina of the eye (humans have three cone types). Thus hamsters can see in shades of green and yellow, which helps them find their special feed. On the other hand, they recognize red with great difficulty. Researchers use hamsters' poor red sensitivity to advantage by keeping the golden hamster under weak red light at night in the breeding areas; the light helps the researcher gather information, but the hamsters hardly notice it.

How well hamsters hear

The hamsters' hearing is much better developed than their eyesight. Besides normal hearing, hamsters can, like bats, hear in the ultrasound range. The sounds uttered in mating and for defense occur in this range. High sounds from the environment, like the rattling of a pile of dishes, disturb the animals terribly and should be avoided as much as possible.

The outstanding sense of smell

The hamsters' sense of smell is probably their best developed sense. Through scent, the animals are able to send information among themselves, such as their sex, their readiness to mate, their relationship, or their territory. Besides being transmitted in urine and stool, scents are delivered by special glands. Golden hamster females mainly deposit scent markings with their vagina, while males mark their territories by means of glands in their sides.

If you carefully take a golden hamster in your hand and blow sideways on its fur,

TEST

Would a Hamster Be a Good Pet for Me?

Hamsters are interesting, but they are not cuddly animals. Therefore, you should make certain a hamster will fit into your life.

	Yes	No
1. Are you sure you don't want to have an animal you can cuddle?	○	○
2. Do you know that hamsters don't like to be handled?	○	○
3. Do you enjoy watching the natural behavior of animals?	○	○
4. Can you offer the hamster a big cage?	○	○
5. Will you furnish the cage with lots of variety?	○	○
6. Are you ready to offer the hamster frequent free runs out of the cage?	○	○
7. Do you know that the hamster only has an average life expectancy of about two to three years?	○	○
8. Are you prepared to give your hamster daily care?	○	○
9. Will you feed it a varied diet of grains, fruits, and vegetables as well as protein food?	○	○
10. Do you know someone who can look after your hamster if you are away?	○	○

ANSWERS: If you could answer all questions with Yes, then a hamster is exactly the right pet for you. If you answered with even one No, you should consider whether you would be happy with a hamster or if you should decide on getting another pet.

Simplified Food Search

▶ **1** **By means of the tactile hairs,** the vibrissae, the hamster is able to "take the measure" of narrow openings precisely.

▶ **2** **The nose** of the hamster is its most important organ of sense, not just for hunting food.

▶ **3** **Hoarding** is typical for the little pet. Large quantities of food are carried into its little house.

these black glands can be seen. On the other hand, dwarf hamsters are endowed with ventral glands, which are located on the belly side. Hamsters perceive the smell of feed and other things with the scent cells in the nose. Beyond that, they have a special organ in their head, the vomeronasal organ, with which information about fellow species members like sex, breeding readiness, and degrees of relationship is perceived. The hamsters mainly orient themselves in the terrain by using scent, but they obviously do not depend solely on the sense of smell for that. This is shown by experiments in which the orientation of golden hamsters is tested in mazes. For example, researchers created a maze based on the model of the one in the royal palace garden at Hampton Court in London. A hamster, placed in the center of the maze, had to find his way out. As a reward, he received a piece of food or was allowed back in his home cage. So that the animals couldn't orient themselves by smell, the maze was washed down with vinegar after each run. In spite of this procedure, the animals very quickly learned to find their way around in the maze. One assumes that in practice they register the sequence of movements and store them in their brain like a map.

What hamsters feel

Of course, hamsters can perceive touches over their entire skin surface and react very fearfully, for example, when they are grabbed in their sleep. Tactile hairs in the muzzle area (vibrissae) are important for their orientation to the terrain. These hairs signal unevenness of the ground under their feet, especially at dusk. With the vibrissae—better than with their eyes—they can detect drop-offs and step back. The vibrissae are especially practical in the building of the burrow, allowing the hamsters to register the size of their chambers and the passageways in the darkness.

Habits

Even when living with humans, hamsters remain wild animals and have adapted their natural behavior only slightly for domestic living.

Hamsters are loners

All hamster species live alone, that is, as singles. This means that all hamsters keep out of each other's way as much as possible! Only during mating do the male and the female meet for a short time. Among golden hamsters, the mother raises her children alone and does not tolerate the father in their vicinity. Among dwarf hamsters, there is no concrete evidence about the participation of the male in the raising of the young.

Note: Be very careful about putting hamsters together! The introduction of two hamsters that do not know each other can lead to aggressive conflicts, depending on the species. If the subordinate animal cannot get out of the cage, it is often attacked for so long that it can die of its injuries.

The hamster burrow

The burrow of the golden hamster lies about 39 in. (1 m) under the earth's surface and usually has only one vertical entrance with a diameter of 1 to 2 in. (4 to 5 cm). This main tunnel goes straight down to a depth of about 12 in. (30 cm). In winter or in times of great

TIP

Please do not disturb!

Hamsters react very sensitively to tactile stimuli. Therefore, sleeping animals should never be touched. This causes great stress on them. If the hamster is hand tamed, you may be able to take it in hand or, while on the floor, stroke it with a finger. Avoid touching the hamster on the belly!

How well does your hamster learn and see?

Divide a shoebox in half horizontally with a glued-in cardboard wall. Cut two openings in one long side. Each half can then be entered through an opening. Put a black circle over one door and a triangle over the other and set it up so that you can change the symbols.

The test begins:

In the half with the triangle, place scentless dry food and let the hamster go. Note where it goes in first. When the hamster has found the food, repeat the test several times. Change the symbols over the doors according to the halves where the food is. However, the food must always remain behind the same symbol. Does your hamster recognize the shapes and does it learn to choose the right door?

My test results:

drought, the entrance is closed with a clump of earth. Temperature measurements in the earth showed a consistent temperature in spring of about 53°F (12°C), so the hamster can protect itself from heat and cold there. At a depth of about 23 in. (60 cm), there is a 4- to 8-in. (10- to 20-cm)-wide nest chamber, which is usually cushioned with dried plant material. From this nest chamber, two tunnels lead to one chamber for storing food and another toilet chamber for waste. But the food may also be stored in several chambers. Researchers have discovered that there are no differences between the burrows of males and females.

Also with golden hamsters that are kept as pets, you can determine that the animal always uses the same corner of the cage for its intended purpose.

The day begins at night

There are many studies of the daily activities of the hamster, but these are done with caged animals, not those in the wild. According to the studies, hamsters are nocturnal and begin to awaken from their day's sleep in the evening hours or with the onset of twilight. Then they are awake all night. Hamsters are particularly active about three hours after they wake up. They do not settle down and sleep again until morning.

We have recently gained entirely new information about the activity of golden hamsters living in the wild. Observations of them in their burrows in spring have shown that the animals leave the burrow about an hour before dusk and then vanish into the burrow when it gets dark. After sunrise the next morning, they can once more be observed outside the burrow for about an hour after which they gradually withdraw into their holes again.

Over the course of the year, after passing the entire winter in the burrow, golden hamsters reemerge into daylight in the beginning of March. Also, the animals appear to remain in their burrows during the hot summer months from June to September.

Life expectancy

Like most small mammals, hamsters have a high metabolism, since it is difficult for them to maintain their body temperature (average 99.5°F [37.5C°]). So the small heart of the golden hamster beats 325 times per minute on average (compared to humans' 70 beats per minute). This contributes to the fact that hamsters have such a short life expectancy. For the golden hamster, it amounts to about two years, three at most. In the wild, most hamsters probably do not survive the second winter.

Hibernation

Golden hamsters differ from dwarf hamsters, who do not actually go to sleep, so-called facultative hibernators. Golden hamsters in the wild enter into winter sleep when the temperature sinks below about 46°F (8°C). Inside their burrows, they roll themselves into a ball to keep from losing their body heat. The body temperature will gradually sink to about 86°F (30°C), which slows breathing and causes the heart to beat only two or three times per minute. During this period the hamsters live on their reserves, which are stored in the special brown fat tissue in their shoulder and neck region. A hibernating hamster appears to be lifeless because it does not react to stimuli such as touch. However, if the animal is placed in a warmer environment, it gradually begins to move. The front part of the body is the first to be acti-

---

Fresh branches are attractive, and hamsters try everything to get at the healthy greens.
▼

vated; the belly and the rear legs take a little longer to react. The animals awaken about every five days during their two to three months of winter sleep to eat extensively of the food supplies they have stored in their burrow. Hamsters that are kept as pets should not fall into hibernation, and you should never under any circumstances provoke it. Keep in mind that going into hibernation, as well as waking up, always places the greatest stresses on the animal's organism. Its already brief life expectancy will be further diminished by this behavior.

Hamster Behavior

Since hamsters live solitary lives, they do not have the extensive repertoire of behaviors found in animals that live in social groups. The following text describes the characteristic behaviors of the golden hamster kept singly and when he or she is confronted with an

In unfamiliar surroundings, hamsters always stand up to better take in environmental stimuli.
▼

unfamiliar creature. Hamster behavior during the mating season is dealt with in the chapter on hamster mating and birth of the young beginning on page 109.

▶ Running: The hamster runs around in the cage, mainly using its nose to orient itself. It puts its nose to the floor in a quick succession of sniffs. Frantic activity indicates hunger or looking for food.

▶ Resting: The hamster lies all rolled up in its nest. The lower the temperature outside, the more perfect the ball shape. At high temperatures, the hamster stretches out more and more, in order to cool itself.

▶ Crawling: The hamster feels threatened or is uncertain and thus presses its body to the floor so as not to be seen.

▶ Exploring behavior: The hamster puts its nose to the floor at short intervals and inspects surroundings. From time to time, it stands up.

▶ Sudden stopping, rising onto the hind legs: The hamster is taking in stimuli such as sounds or smells in the environment.

▶ Displacement grooming: Environmental stimuli make the hamster uneasy. However, it does not know how it should behave—go on or flee? The energy released is "displaced" and "discharges" itself as "anxiety gestures" in grooming movements. Anxiety gestures can also be observed in humans who have to talk in front of large audiences (e.g., they play with a pencil).

▶ Comfort behavior: Extensive grooming with the front paws (with both at once or alternately).

- Stretching and yawning: The hamster is completely relaxed and does not feel threatened.
- Teeth chattering: This is a sign of impending aggression and can be observed, for example, after a confrontation with an unfamiliar hamster.
- Aggression: The hamster snarls and tries to bite its opponent.
- Submissive behavior: The subordinate hamster lays back its ears, first

throw themselves on their backs and squeak when one tries to take hold of them.

DID YOU KNOW THAT...

. . . hamsters can hear and smell extremely well?

Smell and hearing are the hamster's most important senses. Golden hamsters can recognize individuals by scent. Experiments have shown that even siblings that have grown up separated will recognize each other again. Besides the sounds that we humans can hear, hamsters communicate in the ultrasound range. Young hamsters give out so-called desolation sounds in the ultrasound range very soon after birth, for example, if it's too cold. The mother hears this "cry for help" very clearly. But the sounds will not be perceived by any predators that may seek out the young. Incidentally, it appears that hamsters can also differentiate among voice sounds. For example, if you always use certain words in greeting the little pet, it will soon recognize you by your voice.

lifts a front paw in side position, and then throws itself onto its back. It then presents its vulnerable underside, intending to diminish the biting inhibition in the other hamster.

- Squeaking and shrieking: Hamsters use these expressions of pain, for instance, after being severely bitten in an attack. Young, untamed hamsters

AN OVERVIEW OF THE DIFFERENT HAMSTER SPECIES

	Syrian Golden Hamster (Mesocricetus auratus)	Campbell's Dwarf Hamster (Phodopus campbelli)
Geographical distribution	Northern Syria, southern Turkey	Mongolia, Altai Mountains, small areas in northeast China
Habitat	Farm fields, steppes	Semideserts, steppes
Body weight	Up to 6.4 oz (180 g): average: male 5.3 oz (150 g), female 4.7 oz (133 g)	Up to 1.8 oz (50 g), on average 0.9–1.1 oz (25–30 g)
Metabolic adaptations	Hibernation below approx. 46°F (8°C) and fewer than 10 hr light per day	No hibernation; at surrounding temperature of 14°F (–10°C) the body temperature decreases to 74.7°F (23.7°C)
Rhythm of activity	Outside the burrow for approx. 2 hr in evening and morning twilight; as a pet, nocturnally active	Active at twilight and at night
Sexual cycle (length of estrus)	4 days; estrus 16 hours (from beginning of darkness until midday the next day)	4 days; estrus like the golden hamster
Reproduction period	March to November	Middle or end of April to the end of September
Term of pregnancy	16 days	18 days
Litter size	Up to 14 young, average litter size 8 young	Up to 9 young, average litter size 6 young
Sexual maturity	Male at 40–50 days, female at 30 days	At about 45 days
Burrow	A 1.6– to 2-in. (4– to 5-cm)-wide entrance, a vertical tunnel approx. 19.7 in. (50 cm) deep, nest chamber, at least one storeroom	4–6 vertical and horizontal tunnels that lead to the nest chamber; also uses the burrows of the gerbil

Djungarian (or Striped Hairy-footed) Dwarf Hamster (*Phodopus sungorus*)	Roborovski Dwarf Hamster (*Phodopus roborovskii*)	Chinese Hamster (*Cricetulus griseus*)
Steppes of western Siberia and eastern Kazakstan, steppes of the Krasnoyarsk region of Russia	Eastern Kazakhstan, Mongolia, eastern and western borderlands of China	Northeastern China
Steppes, semideserts, wheat and alfalfa fields, also forests, meadows, and birch stands	Semideserts and sandy wastes; sand-loving	Semideserts and sandy wastes; sand-loving
Male: 0.7–1.6 oz (19–45 g), females 0.7–1.3 oz. (19–36 g)	0.7–0.9 oz (20–25 g)	1.1–1.6 oz (30–45 g)
No hibernation, but torpor (fluffed up and huddling together on short days below 68°F (20°C), decrease in body weight and food intake)	No hibernation, no torpor; however, activity decreases severely with onset of the cold season	No hibernation
Active at night and dusk	Active at night and dusk	Active at night and dusk
4 days, estrus like the golden hamster	4 days, estrus like the golden hamster	Not yet known
April/May to September; in Kazakstan can also reproduce in winter	April/May to September	April/May to September
18 days	18 days	20–22 days
Up to 12 young, average litter size 6 young	3–8 young, average litter size 4 young	2–12 young
40–45 days	About 30 days	About 30 days
Several horizontal and vertical tunnels come together in a main tunnel	Nearly straight tunnels, 19.7–39.4 in. (50–100 cm) long; broaden at end to a circular nest chamber	Summer: vertical tunnels 19.7–39.4 in. (50–100 cm) long with round nest chambers at the end; winter: branching burrow system

Portraits
of Breeds at a Glance

◀ Golden Hamster

Despite their long "careers" as pets, hamsters still continue to exhibit the same behaviors as their relatives living in the wild. They have only slightly adapted to human beings. However, with good care, most hamsters that are kept as pets will live longer than their wild cousins.

Original Form ▶

The golden hamster in its natural coloration has a red-brown back and a white belly. Although this species has been kept as a house pet for 75 years, it cannot be distinguished from its fellow species members living in the wild. Wild-colored golden hamsters quickly become tame with frequent human contact, so they are very suitable for beginning hamster keepers.

▲ Color Variation

This beautiful variant has a light gray base color and black spots.

▲ Color Variation

Hamsters are now bred in many colors. In the simplest instance, bicolored hamsters have brown fur and have more or less large white patches on their coats.

Color Variation ▶

Another color variation of the hamster. This example has a white base color with black spots.

▲ Russian Hamster

It has a white base color with blackish colorations on nose, ears, tail, and feet.

Single-Colored Golden Hamster

This golden hamster has pure white fur and normal eye color. Albinos with white fur have red eyes. The single-colored golden hamsters are very similar to the wild form in temperament.

Color Variation

This black-and-white hamster has a particularly strong contrasting coat coloration.

Color Variation ▶

This golden hamster has three coat colors: black, white, and brown. Compared to the wild form, hamsters with color variations are more difficult to keep. They are usually more aggressive and easily frightened; therefore, they are also harder to tame than their wild-colored fellow hamsters.

Black Golden Hamster

This single-colored black breed form of the golden hamster is said to be, like all single-colored forms, quite robust and easy to care for.

Long-Haired Golden Hamster

Golden hamsters with long fur are also called teddy bear hamsters. The long coat gets dirty or matted easily and thus requires regular grooming. Long-haired hamsters are not suitable for beginning hamster keepers because of the time-consuming grooming.

Satin Hamster ▶

This gray satin hamster has a plush coat. Long-haired and satin hamsters are generally considered quite good-natured and easily tamed.

Satin Hamster

Here is a red-brown variant of the satin hamster. Because of its silky fur, it is very popular with hamster lovers.

◀ Roborovski Dwarf Hamster

This is the smallest of the three hamster species that are described in this book. Roborovski dwarf hamsters are said to be shy and very difficult to tame. One can, however, observe them from a distance.

▲

Roborovski Dwarf Hamster

The half-pint among the hamsters only grows to $1\frac{1}{2}$–2 in. (4–5 cm) in size.

▲

Djungarian Dwarf Hamster

The dark color of this pretty hamster almost corresponds to the wild form. This species, as well as Campbell's dwarf hamsters, are relatively easy to keep.

▲

Djungarian Dwarf Hamster

There are also color and pattern variations in the small hamster species as shown here in this Djungarian dwarf hamster.

Chinese Striped Hamster ▶

The Chinese striped hamster belongs to the genus of the long-haired dwarf hamsters. Their little tails, about 1 in. (2–3 cm) long, are an important identifying characteristic. Altogether, the little rodent gets to be about 4–5 in. (10–13 cm) in size. Chinese striped hamsters have very strong genetic wild animal behaviors and are difficult to tame.

Campbell's Dwarf Hamster

The color on their backs tends to be browner than that of the Djungarian dwarf hamster. The boundary between the back and the belly is light brown.

▼

▲

Chinese Dwarf Hamster

The back stripe of the Chinese hamster is especially pronounced. Therefore it is also known as the striped hamster.

How Hamsters Like to Live

Hamsters want to be able to run, love to climb, and withdraw to sleep. Therefore you need space, an interestingly constructed home, and a little sleep house.

Where the Hamster Feels Comfortable

Now it's a matter of creating a home for the hamster where it truly feels at home. If you bear in mind the little animal's living conditions in the wild, it will not be that difficult to offer it a comfortable home.

If you were able to answer all the questions on the test on page 15, "Would a hamster be a good pet for me?" with an honest "yes," nothing more stands in the way of your keeping the little mammal. Of course the primary factors contributing to its good health are optimal living conditions, those that are completely in tune with the small rodent's special requirements.

The Right Place for the Hamster Cage

The first question you have to ask is: Where is my hamster going be the most comfortable in my house?

Cage location: As already noted, the hamster likes to sleep in the daytime when we are active. So an ideal place is in a room that is not used frequently during the day. If that is not possible and you also want to look into the hamster cage every now and then, you should find a quiet corner in the living room or the children's room. The hamster is very sensitive to shaking and high-frequency sounds, such as those caused by a television set or a computer that is always on. Since the animals do not close their eyes nor can their pupils narrow, constant bright light is unbearable for them. Therefore, even though the hamster will withdraw into its little house to rest, the location of the cage should not be too bright. So a place near the window is not suitable. Since you will later sit in front of the cage to observe your little housemate, the cage should be at about eye level. This naturally depends on the size of the observers. A small table or chest at least 27 in. (70 cm) high has proven to be ideal. Two sides of the cage should be opaque. If it is not possible to back the cage against a wall, I recommend that you darken the sides.

The "hamster rocker" is one of many accessories that are available in the pet store. You can keep dwarf hamsters busy with a rocker like this, too.

2 **The cage** absolutely must be large enough to permit the introduction of many accessories. A sleeping house to retire into is especially important.

▼

▲

1 **The wooden bridge** serves as climbing equipment and permits a comfortable ascent into the cage after a free run.

▲

3 **Tasty treats** that are hung in the cage create variety in the menu. However, they should not contain any sugar.

Room Temperature: The temperature in the room can be 59–77°F (15–25°C) and, if possible, should not exceed that. Lower temperatures for a short time are not problematic; however, higher temperatures stress the rodent's metabolism enormously. Therefore, you should never, ever place the cage in the sun or in the vicinity of the heating unit. Look instead for a spot in the house that is shady with even temperatures. Obviously, the temperature must not drop below freezing. As already noted, golden hamsters begin to hibernate below 46°F (8°C). This transformation severely stresses the animal and should therefore be avoided at all costs.

Dwarf hamsters also remain active at low temperatures (even below freezing), in contrast to the golden hamsters, and do not go into hibernation.

With Djungarian dwarf hamsters, the coat changes into their white winter coat at prolonged low temperatures. If the cage is placed in a room that is unheated in winter, you must make sure that the humidity never rises above 70 percent (measured with a humidistat), to avoid conditions promoting colds. Be especially careful not to let the cage be situated near a draft, and refrain from smoking in the hamster room at all times.

The Comfortable Home for Small Rodents

In order to maintain a hamster properly, the first matter of importance is of course the size of the living area. In principle, the cage cannot be big enough. If you look out for the largest suitable cage you can find for your hamster, then, and only then, will it feel comfortable and show you its entire repertoire of interesting behaviors. **Least possible size:** Although cages are available in varying sizes, the one for a golden hamster should have a surface area of at least 465 square in. (3000 square cm). This equals a measure of 32 in. (80 cm) wide and 16 in. (40 cm) deep. Keep in mind that a large part of the cage will be taken up by the hamster's sleep house. The height of the cage should measure at least 16 in. (40 cm) high. With dwarf hamsters, the cage can be somewhat smaller, but here also the dimensions of the ground area should be no less than 12×32 in. (30×80 cm).

Cage levels: An increase of cage space by the installation of additional levels connected with little ladders or ramps is highly recommended. This greatly improves the well-being of all hamsters, since both golden and dwarf hamsters are true master climbers. Of course these additional levels should not be made of wire screen or grating. The little animals cannot be expected to walk on such a surface with their delicate paws. Hamster feet are designed for walking on the ground. They will slide off wires, and injuries are inevitable. The height of the "floors" must allow the animals to stand up, and thus for the golden hamster they must be at least 8 in. (20 cm) high. Cages with such levels already installed are available commercially in select stores.

Cage or Glass Aquarium?

Both cages and glass aquariums have advantages and disadvantages, which will be explained in detail on the following pages. So, what factors need to be taken into consideration?

A cage as a comfortable home

Advantages and disadvantages: Wire cages have the advantage of good air circulation, which hinders the collection of noxious gases and, to some degree, slows the spoilage of fresh food. On the other hand, with this sort of cage, special care must be taken to ensure that the hamster is never, ever placed in a draft (see page 32).

Floor pan: The floor of the cage is a plastic pan, which should be about 3–4 in. (8–10 cm) deep. The color of the floor pan is left to your own personal taste. It doesn't affect the hamster's sense of well-being (see Sight, page 14). But keep in mind that the hamster likes to scratch holes in the litter and often pushes it together in one place in the cage. So a deeper tray will help keep the litter from falling out, but of course it

> **TIP**
>
> ### Keeping a hamster in an apartment
>
> If you live in an apartment, you may need to ask your landlord for permission to keep small animals like hamsters. This is part of the agreed-upon use of the apartment. The landlord will need to make sure that there is no burden placed on the other tenants by the keeping of hamsters.

limits your view of the animal even more. You can help by lining one of the shallower cage pans with a strip of acrylic or Plexiglas around the top of the pan. You can easily find the material under the term "glass for hobby projects" in a building supply store. You can also get it cut to the desired size right there. You need two pieces each for the

should run horizontally. This way the hamster can climb on them extensively (the hamster runs a comparatively small risk of getting its limbs pinched). In order to further rule out such injuries, the space between bars should be no less than ½ in. (12 mm) for golden hamsters, ⅓ in. (7 mm) for the dwarf hamsters.

The cage bars should be made of galvanized steel wire. Painted wire or wire coated with a layer of plastic is not suit-

DID YOU KNOW THAT . . .

. . . hamsters spend an enormous amount of time in their burrows?

Golden hamsters spend approximately 20 hours of the day in their burrows in the springtime. They only come out in the morning and evening twilight, looking for food. When the temperature rises sharply in summer or sinks in the fall, golden hamsters are not seen outside their burrows for months at a time. So it is clearly very important for your hamster to have an undisturbed place. For hamsters living with us as pets, housing arrangements must always include a little house for sleeping and retiring. Long, undisturbed sleep is a life-supporting necessity for the hamster, who is active for hours at a time at night. Hamsters for whom no sleeping house is provided often become aggressive, tend to get sick more often, and have a shorter life expectancy.

long sides and the short sides, and they should be about 4 in. (10 cm) high. Drill two holes at each end of the strips in order to fasten the acrylic or Plexiglas strips around the cage above the floor tray with wire (from hardware supply store).

Cage bars: The arrangement of the cage bars is very important. The bars

able for hamsters. The hamster will gnaw away both types of coatings within a short time, especially in the corners, and these areas will begin to rust.

Cage door: It's convenient for cleaning or for feeding if the cage can be opened from the top as well as from the front.

Usually your hamster is happy with a **big cage.** When the equipment inside offers a lot of variation, there is no risk of boredom.

An aquarium as a comfortable home

Advantages and disadvantages: Perhaps you are thinking of setting up a retired, leaky aquarium as a hamster home. In principle, there's nothing against using one; however, the requirement for a minimum size is even more important here than with a cage. Aquariums are entirely enclosed. Therefore, air circulation is greatly restricted in such a container. Gaseous ammonia is released from the hamster's urine and can occur in especially high concentrations if you do not clean the aquarium regularly. Ammonia puts unnecessary stress on the little rodent's respiratory organs. Heat exchange is decreased in an aquarium as well. Another disadvantage is that it is difficult to clean. The aquarium must be entirely washed out or rinsed, which is of course very complicated. At the same time, though, aquariums also have several advantages. The hamsters are always sheltered from noises and drafts. This makes aquariums especially appealing for pregnant females and the raising of their young because the animals react even more sensitively to disturbances than normal at this time. Additionally, no litter falls out, and the animals cannot injure themselves on the cage bars. If you keep the glass clean, you can observe the animals better than in a wire cage.

Size: An aquarium that is going to house a golden hamster must be at least 39 in. (100 cm) long and 16 in. (40 cm) deep. For dwarf hamsters, which are, by the way, the best for keeping in an aquarium, the sides should be at least 32 in. (80 cm) high.

Covering: To permit sufficient entry of air, aquariums must never be covered too tightly on top. It would be ideal to simply leave the container open at the top. For golden hamsters, this is only possible if a minimum distance of 12 in. (30 cm) to the upper edge of the container can be maintained, taking into account the equipment (sleeping house, exercise wheel, etc.). The escape artists will try to reach the upper edge of the container with little jumps, especially in the corners. One chin-up is enough to put your little pet on the outside.

Is that edible? The hamster can rely on its sensitive nose.

▼

I recommend a cover of window-screening stretched over a frame of wooden strips about ¾ in. (2 cm) wide. Vented "aquarium toppers" are also available in most pet stores and online. **Note:** The glass in older aquarium frames may be put together with red lead. The modern silicon adhesives are largely harmless to hamsters, but lead is not.

Additional levels in the cage expand the walkable surface and creative variety. It is important that the floors be made of wood and not metal bars.

▼

Equipment and More...

Would you be comfortable in a home that did not have certain basic furniture? Of course not. Similarly, your hamster requires some basic comforts too. With a sleeping house, litter, and nest-building material, your hamster can make a home.

You can also produce an acrylic hamster home, similar to the glass aquarium. The pieces of acrylic should be glued with a nontoxic adhesive. Such containers are lighter than glass aquariums and are easier to clean. Their disadvantage is that the panes gradually become dulled or scratched, which naturally impedes your view of your little friend.

A terrarium as hamster home

In addition to aquariums, terrariums, sold in pet stores, also can be used to house small rodents and reptiles. They have the advantage of built-in ventilation systems. In addition, ventilation grills are usually set at the front bottom and back top so that the air can circulate throughout the entire container. Take care, however, to make sure that the lower ventilation grill does not get covered by litter.

The "Homemade Brand" Cage

A self-built hamster home is appropriate for the animal. If you have even a little skill in building things and have some tools, you should not hesitate to go to work. The suggested hamster

home consists of a wooden cage with a front pane of acrylic and a floor pan. **Floor pan:** It is made of plastic and placed in the finished cage as the bottom. Minimum size: 16×32 in. (40×80 cm); height: 3–4 in. (8–10 cm) (see page 33). If you can't find a pan like this, you must build it yourself. At the building supply store, have a piece of 5 mm ($\frac{1}{5}$ in.) acrylic (Plexiglas) cut for a floor piece (e.g., 20×39 in. [50×100 cm]) and two long sides (20×39 in. [50×100 cm]) and two side pieces (4×20 in. [10×50 cm]). **Constructing the floor pan:** Using nontoxic adhesive, glue the side strips first and then the front and back strips to the floor piece. The floor pan, and thus the cage insert, is finished.

TIP

Softly padded

Hamsters not only carry food into their burrow, but they love to upholster their home with soft stuff. Put two to three pieces of unscented facial tissue or some toilet paper in the cage with your hamster. You will be amazed how quickly the paper is stuffed into its cheek pockets then carried into its "lair."

Our Child Would Like a Hamster

"Our daughter is seven years old and really wants a hamster. However, we think that she is still too young to take care of the animal all by herself. Is keeping hamsters advisable for children?"

Unfortunately the hamster is not a petting animal but rather an animal for observation. It is therefore not suitable for small children. However, your daughter is school age and you can definitely let her have a hamster to take care of—with your help. A child is only ready to care for a small pet on her own at age 11 or 12.

Taking responsibility

Hamsters fit the so-called "little child image": They have a small round head with big button eyes, short little ears, and a small, compact body. Plus there is the cuddly soft fur. Of course adults and children find this droll little hamster sweet and cute. We would love to take it in our hand, press it to us, and stroke it lovingly. Prepare your child for the responsibility he or she would undertake in keeping a hamster and that the child must always take care of the animal, even if he or she has no desire to do it. You should also always be prepared to instruct your child on how to handle the small pet properly and must bear the ultimate responsibility for the animal. If you have several children and they all want a hamster, it would be ideal for each child to have his or her own animal. Therefore they can develop a relationship with "my" hamster and perhaps compete with each other to find out who can care for theirs best. If several children take care of one hamster together, one child may possibly leave the care to the others, or there may be arguments about activities with the hamster. Besides, it has been shown that the hamster can probably differentiate the movements of its owner from those of other people. Thus a constant change will only create stress for the animal.

Advice on buying

Always take your child with you when you buy the animal, so that he or she can make the selection. After all, the goal should be to develop an attachment to the animal. But don't let your child go alone, for he or she will certainly need your advice.

Building the cage: It is best to build your own cage with wooden boards that measure ½–¾ in. (1–2 cm) thick. Washable, coated chipboard is ideal for this purpose. Spruce and pine are not recommended because the wood is very difficult to clean.

First you cut a wooden floor board the size of the floor tray and then glue the two side pieces and the back wall to the floor piece. Minimum height: 24 in. (60 cm). Provide narrow wood strips at the inside front of the side walls as guide tracks for the front wall. In front, at the bottom, place a wooden strip the width of the floor pan inside the guide tracks. Now slide the acrylic front side into the tracks on the side pieces. It closes tightly against the pan, thanks to the wooden strips in the track. This front side can be pulled out for cleaning. Instead of the piece of acrylic, the front could also consist of a frame with small-meshed wire screening stretched over it, which of course has the advantage of better ventilation, but it also harbors

the risk of injury if the hamster gets its small foot caught in the wires.

Cage roof: To cover the cage, use a frame with window screening stretched across it and attach the frame to the back wall with hinges.

Interior equipment: Provide the hamster home with crossbeams, ladders, and other structures (see page 96).

Tube Systems

Hamsters living in their burrows dig tunnels to connect the individual chambers (see page 18). So it is clear that tunnel systems should be integrated into the cage. You can purchase ready-made tubes at your local pet store, or you can make them yourself. Of course, this will again require a little handiwork. So, for example, you could use tubes to connect the cage with a second, smaller cage, which perhaps might then serve as a sleeping space. You will be amazed at how the hamsters love to crawl through these tubes.

One of these cages by itself would be too small for a hamster home. With a short plastic tube, two cages can easily be connected so that the running area for the hamster is doubled.

Connecting: For shorter, horizontal connections up to about 12 in. (30 cm), you can use central vacuum piping or PVC hoses found in builders supply stores. In addition, there are also connecting pieces that you can fit into the cage. The tubes should have an interior diameter of 2 in. (5 cm). Tubes with a somewhat larger diameter can be cleaned more easily but do not have the same effect. Tubes with the smaller diameter, which corresponds to the size of the tunnel in the wild, provide the animals with close body contact with the walls, which obviously gives them a feeling of security and facilitates movement.

For segments of tubing and also, of course, for the tube system altogether, the most suitable is flexible drainage tubing. Its perforations provide good ventilation of the passages. The tubes should be installed so that regular cleaning is possible without any difficulty. Pool supply stores stock 2 in. (5 cm) flexible tubing without perforations.

Note: Vertical tubes or grades steeper than 45 degrees are problematic because the hamster will not gain a foothold to prevent sliding in the smooth tubes.

Cage Litter

The most important function of litter is to absorb the hamster's excretions. Besides that, hamsters love to use it for digging or making nest burrows. Considering the litter's capacity to absorb, you must make sure that it is largely free of dust and pollutants.

The small-animal litter of wood shavings offered in pet stores is still the best.

If the wood shavings litter seems too artificial, you can try bark mulch. However, this litter is not as good for burrowing. Stay away from pine or cedar shavings. They contain a chemical that can cause respiratory problems. Other good choices are aspen pellets, paper pellets, and grass or grain pellets.

Note: Unsuitable are sawdust, garden peat, cat litter, or the like. The dust from these materials can clog the hamster's nostrils or be inhaled into its lungs. This is certain to shorten the little creature's already short life span.

Litter depth: The layer of litter can measure 1–2 in. (3–5 cm). The little burrowers appreciate being able to pursue their instinctive behaviors!

Hay: There should also be a bundle of hay in the hamster home. This has two advantages. Not only does the little animal love to use it for nest building, but the hamster also likes to eat it. Hay's high roughage content prevents diarrheal diseases (see page 84).

Note: Do not ever use so-called cotton fluff! It is not only unnatural, but the hamster can get its extremities caught in its fibers and strangulate. Also avoid coconut fluff and coconut fiber.

The Hamster House

A place for the hamster to retreat to is very important to proper hamster keeping (see Did You Know That . . . , page 34). The little house is often used for hoarding food and should not be too small. A house with a flat roof offers the hamster added opportunities to climb. Although different variants are available commercially, building your own is still the best solution.

The Equipment
at a Glance

Basic equipment

Floor pan, litter, feeding bowl, and drinking bottle as well as a sleeping house are the minimum requirements for a hamster home. Extra floor levels increase the ground surface and provide exercise.

◀ Sleeping House

The best sleeping house is made of wood. For golden hamsters, it should have dimensions of 8 × 4 × 4 in. (20 × 10 × 10 cm) and be provided with a round entrance hole with a diameter of 2 in. (4.5 cm). A fold-back roof is an advantage (see page 42).

◀ Exercise wheel

The exercise wheel should have a diameter of at least 10 in. (25 cm) and a running surface at least 3 in. (8 cm) wide. The running surface should be solid, not made of wire bars. One side of the wheel must be closed (see page 98).

Feeding dish ▶

Feeding dishes of porcelain or pottery are stable and easy to clean. They should have a diameter of 2–2½ in. (5–6 cm) and be about 1 in. (2 cm) high. A rim that slants inward is very desirable.

Sipper water bottle

The sipper water bottle must be easily reachable and should always contain fresh water. The ball-valve closing must allow the hamster a comfortable drink without the water splashing on it.

MY HAMSTER

How and when is your hamster active?

How long is your hamster active? Does it always become alert at the same time? Are there differences depending on the season of the year? Males should be more consistently active than females, whose activity fluctuates in a 4-day rhythm.

The test begins:

Over several days, record the exact time that your hamster leaves its sleeping house and begins to run around the cage. If possible, also write down when it goes to rest. Make a table of the data. If your hamster has an exercise wheel, you can also record how long it is used every day. Ingenious crafters add a small magnet switch to the exercise wheel, which, with a counter available in an electronics store, will even measure the number of turns. How regularly does your hamster use the exercise wheel?

My test results:

Sleeping house dimensions for golden hamsters: A rectangular house for sleeping should have a ground surface of 4 × 8 in. (10 × 20 cm) and be about 4 in. (10 cm) high.

Sleeping house dimensions for dwarf hamsters: For these little hamsters, the sleeping house can be about 1 in. (3 cm) smaller, so about 3 × 6½ in. (7 × 17 cm).

Entry hole: The little house has a round entry less than 1 in. (2 cm) above the floor on one side. For the golden hamster, the diameter of the entry hole comes to about 2 in. (4.5 cm). For the dwarf hamster, the opening should be 1½ in. (3.5 cm) in size. Other openings

such as windows are not provided because hamsters love the dark.

Note: Although little houses of pottery or plastic are also available commercially, I recommend that you select a wooden house. In the plastic houses especially, humidity builds up very quickly, and the animals do not take to them very well. Some pottery houses may be too small for golden hamsters. Pottery houses have some advantages: They can't be easily chewed, they are easier to clean, and they have a relatively heavy weight. Smaller wooden houses are often moved when the hamster tries to get through the entry hole with cheek pockets full. Little houses or igloos of unglazed clay are acceptable, especially for dwarf hamsters. You can easily and safely weight a house with a flat roof with a stone so that it won't move.

Building a wooden sleeping house

An ideal house for your hamster can be quickly made of wooden boards ½–¾ in. (1.5–2 cm) thick glued together with wood glue.

The house is open underneath and is simply placed on the litter. It is practical to have a roof that is removable or that flaps back on hinges. A really clever approach and one that protects the hamster's sleep during any inspection is to have two covers: a transparent acrylic panel with a wooden roof on top of it. Both roofs can be folded back one at a time. Thus, with the wooden roof folded back, the presence or the sleep of the hamster may be inspected unnoticed through the clear panel, since no drafts occur to disturb the animal. If you want to remove spoiling remnants of food, it is easy to fold back the acrylic panel as well.

The Food Bowl

You definitely want to offer your hamster clean food and at the same time have a check on how much it eats. Unfortunately you have made the calculation without the little hamsters. Just like humans who store up more provisions at home than they need for themselves, the practice of "stashing food" is also an inborn behavior of hamsters. Therefore, a feed bowl is really unnecessary when it comes right down to it. However, the strength of the animal's drive to carry all the food possible into a safe place differs very much among each individual animal. Some hamsters

have little interest in hoarding food, while others rush to store every little bit and often keep changing the places where they hide their edible "treasure." Nevertheless, we humans are reluctant to simply throw the food into the cage, so here are some tips on suitable feeding dishes. Using a feeding dish is more hygienic for fresh food and living food than just throwing it on the floor.

The dish should not be too small, but it also should not be so large that the animals can climb into it. If the hamster fits comfortably in the feeding dish, it

A wooden ladder creates variety and in some case encourages acrobatic performances.
▼

The Ideal Resting Place

▶ **1** **A little house** made of wood with a roof that folds back is ideal for golden hamsters. The roof construction allows discreet monitoring.

▶ **2** **Clay igloos** are too small for golden hamsters. But they are suitable for resting places for dwarf hamsters.

▶ **3** **Sleeping houses** of various materials are available. This sisal cone is highly recommended, especially for the little dwarf hamsters.

will naturally soil the food with excrement and urine. So select dishes with a diameter of 2–2½ in. (5–6 cm) and a height of about 1 in. (2 cm), with the rim slanting inward. Dishes of pottery or porcelain are very durable and easy to clean. Plastic dishes tip easily, can be chewed, or get shoved around in the cage.

The Right Water Bottle

Although, as a rule, hamsters in the wild do not drink but get their water requirement exclusively from their fresh food, you should always provide yours in the cage with the possibility of drinking. It is very difficult for you, as keeper, to evaluate whether the hamster has ingested enough water with its food. I recommend a sipper bottle that is installed on the outside of the cage. The mouth of this bottle is closed with a small ball valve. When the hamster drinks, the ball is pushed to the inside, thus making the water available. The

disadvantage of drinking bottles without the ball is that that the narrow drinking tube quickly becomes clogged with calcium salts, especially with hard tap water, and the animal either does not get enough water or gets none at all. Therefore, do not forget to make sure that the water bottle is functioning and to clean it regularly (see page 78). You can also use bottled water to avoid the chlorine. Otherwise, regular drinking water is the proper drink for hamsters. Pet stores sell so-called vitamin drinks, but you can save your money (see page 74).

Note: Do not offer water in an open saucer or, here again, the problem of soiling will occur. Besides, the animal is not used to drinking that way.

The Hamster Toilet

Does it make sense to place a little dish in the cage with sand in it so the hamster can deposit its urine and feces there? There are even little plastic cor-

ner litter pans sold in the pet stores. The answer is a definitive "yes and no." This means that you can try it. In most cases, however, your pet will have its own preference. You will of course find out when cleaning the cage that your hamster always uses the same corner. However, it is rarely the exact one where the toilet dish is located.

"Luxury" Equipment

Many investigations by behavioral researchers have determined how vital it is for the animals' well-being to enrich their cages with materials for exploring or hiding. It is therefore no "luxury" to offer your pet facilities for its innate behavioral repertoire. More details about such facilities can be found in the chapter on activity and wellness (see from page 94). Suitable objects are ones made of natural materials like wood, sisal, bark, or straw. If you cannot find anything appropriate in the stores, call on your own improvisational

capacities. Then you might bring "joy" to your hamster with small boxes of unprinted cardboard into which you have cut holes.

TIP

Snug nest

Hamsters like to pad their nests to make them cozy. Therefore, you should spread out "upholstery materials" in the cage for your hamster to collect. Besides hay (see page 66), suitable materials are straw, thin branches, unscented paper tissues, toilet paper, or pieces of brown wrapping paper. That way your little friend will stay busy and be cozy at the same time.

Questions About Shelter and Equipment

? What is the minimum size of the hamster cage?

For the golden hamster the cage should be at least 32 in. (80 cm), and for dwarf hamsters at least 24 in. (60 cm) long. The minimum cage depth for the golden hamster is 16 in. (40 cm) and for the dwarf hamster 12 in. (30 cm). For all species, the cage should be at least 16 in. (40 cm) high, although a taller cage allows installation of a middle story, which is very desirable. Incidentally, the cage can never be too large.

? What should I keep in mind when choosing equipment for my hamster?

Objects of natural materials such as wood, cork, bark, sisal, cardboard, or even stone are most suitable. If possible, they should not be printed or painted. Plastics or rather plastic equipment items are less suitable.

? Can I make equipment out of packing material (Styrofoam)?

I would advise against it. Packing material is of course very light and can be worked relatively easily. But that is also a disadvantage. Your hamster will quickly chew through it. Although the material is not poisonous of itself, the animal can eat it and get intestinal blockage.

? Do hamsters need a drinking bottle?

Yes. Even though hamsters in the wild hardly drink at all, they do take up the morning dew, among other liquids. Since one cannot always estimate the water content of the juicy food and perhaps it isn't available all the time, there should always be a bottle of fresh water in the cage.

? Is a water dish advisable?

No, I advise against it. Besides rapid soiling of the water, it has happened that the animals (especially dwarf hamsters) have drowned in it.

? How should the hamster's sleeping house actually be made?

For golden hamsters, the base of the sleeping house should measure about 4 × 8 in. (10 × 20 cm); for dwarf hamsters, 3 × 6½ in. (7 × 17 cm). The height should be about 4 in. (10 cm). The entrance to the little house must be 2 in. (4.5 cm) for golden hamsters; for dwarf hamsters a 1½-in. (3.5-cm) wide entry is enough. You should choose wood above all other materials. A fold-back roof attached with hinges is the best. This makes inspection of the house and removal of the previous day's hoarded fresh food much easier. Besides, it allows the hamster to remain almost undisturbed.

❓ Can I paint my home-made wooden cage to make maintaining it easier?

Yes, that's possible. However, use only solvent-free, water-based (nontoxic) paint. Get advice at the building supply or paint stores.

❓ Can I join several cages with pipes or tubing?

Yes, of course, this is even recommended, since the hamster gains such varied living conditions with a larger ground surface. The pipe should be aerated, however, and have an interior diameter of almost 2 in. (4.5 cm). Flexible drain pipe is good for the purpose. Drill holes in PVC tubing (from a building supply store) at intervals of about 2 in. or more (5 cm) for ventilation. Also, home-made passages made of wooden lattice (above and below) with Plexiglas or acrylic side walls can be comfortably used by the hamster and, at the same time, allows you to observe him or her. Be sure that the lattice isn't cedar or pressure-treated wood.

❓ What bottom layer (litter) should I choose?

Here good old wood shavings are the first recommendation, with the exception of pine or cedar, which can cause respiratory problems. Finer material can be inhaled by the animals, and it can stick to their nostrils. Other litter choices are aspen, paper, grass, or grain pellets. The height of the litter should be a little more than 1 in. (3 cm).

❓ Can I decorate my hamster home with artificial plants?

No, that is not ideal because the animals gnaw on the plants. Since it is very often not known what material the artificial plants are made of, they can endanger the health of your hamster. Besides, they become dirty or dusty with time. Natural plants have no place in the hamster cage either. They can be poisonous for the hamster.

❓ I do not want my hamster to run on the floor during free exercise. What can I do?

The most suitable surface for free running is an old linen cloth, for example, or a bed sheet. Other materials are also suitable; however, make sure there is a smooth surface. Old hand towels or bath towels made of terrycloth are not suitable, since the hamster can get its little toes caught in the threads. The great advantage of a large piece of cloth as the bottom surface is that at the end of the free run you can roll up the cloth along with the bits of shavings or feces left behind. A rigid surface of, say, plastic, does not have this advantage. Besides, it is hard for your hamster to run on plastic.

Welcome Home

It is done. You have made your choice and your little friend can move in with you. You need to start creating trust with patience and dedication so that everything goes well from the beginning.

A Good Buy Is a Well Considered One

The hamster home is ready, and you can hardly wait to install your new companion. But now where are you going to get your "dream hamster" and what must you keep in mind when buying your small pet?

Where Do You Find the Hamster of Your Dreams?

There are four places to find the hamster of your choice:
- From the breeder,
- From the pet store,
- From friends and acquaintances,
- From an animal shelter.

From the breeder

If you know of a hamster breeder in your area, this is the best option for getting the hamster of your dreams. Even having to go a little distance should not put you off. It would be balanced by many advantages. Usually with a breeder you have a large choice among the different breeds, can get good advice, and can certainly get some tips for successful maintenance and care at the same time. If you have fallen in love with a particular breed, as a rule the only path for you is the one to the breeder. Another great advantage is that the breeder can tell you the exact day when the hamster will be born. So you can not only celebrate the little creature's birthday but also know exactly how old your pet is. You will find addresses of breeders on the Internet.

Sometimes breeders also advertise in trade journals (see page 141). In any case, you should visit the breeder in person. Under no circumstances should the animal be sent by mail. A serious breeder would not do this anyway.

From the pet store

Perhaps you have already visited several pet stores in your area and noticed that there are differences. But don't buy in the very first store—compare them! Go into the store that makes the best impression on you. It should give you the feeling that the animals are properly looked after. The cages are clean and

Dwarf hamsters are really easy to care for, but they do not become tame as quickly as the golden hamster, for instance.

not too crowded. The animals should act the way their species is supposed to. They should have sleeping quarters, which are not too brightly lighted. Obviously the cages should not be sitting in the display window.

The feeding bowls and the drinking bottles should not be dirty, and the animals should have enough to eat. Talk with the pet dealer and ask for advice. You can tell from the answers to your questions whether he or she is dealing with you seriously, if the dealer has the necessary competence and takes time to speak with you.

From private people

Do you have a friend, colleague, or relative whose hamster has had babies? If you know him or her well, you know whether the animals have been properly cared for and are healthy. Here, too, you will find out when your charge was born, how big the litter was, and what behavioral characteristics the mother might have had. The disadvantage is that you have a limited choice and must be satisfied with the given breed.

From the animal shelter

If you have decided to get a hamster from an animal shelter, you are certainly doing a good work. You are allowing the animal to have the existence it deserves for the rest of its life. Most are older animals whose keepers—perhaps children—have lost interest in them. Or a long vacation was coming and no one

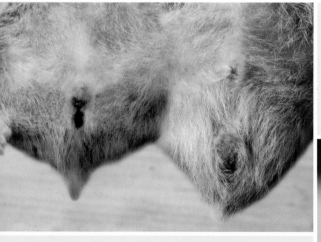

1 **Sex determination:** In females (left) the distance between the anus and the genital opening is smaller than in the male (right). The testicles of the male emerge in summertime.

2 **The determining of sex** is particularly difficult in young hamsters, such as here with a three-week-old animal. In this case, you had best consult an expert such as a breeder or a veterinarian.

Hamsters in the original wild colors are most suitable for beginning hamster keepers. ▶

was willing take over the care of the hamster. Animal shelters have an advantage: These animals are usually tame, so you can gain your first experiences in hamster keeping easily. It is especially good for children when the hamster has already had a great deal of contact with humans.

The Right Time to Buy

The time of day you visit your future companion is not entirely without significance. Hamsters are active at dusk and rest in their little houses during the day. When they are abruptly snatched from sleep, they react with stress and usually try to bite in self-defense. Then, of course, it is difficult to look the animal over carefully and to make judgments about coloring or the condition of health. Therefore, the best time for buying a hamster is the last hour before the business closes, when the animals are at the beginning of their natural activity period. At this time, they leave their sleeping houses of their own accord and exhibit their normal behavior patterns.

Which Hamster Is the Best?

Take plenty of time when buying the hamster in a pet shop. You should definitely plan on 20 or 30 minutes. Watch the animals quietly for a quarter of an hour. Do they all exhibit hamster-like behavior or does your animal fall into the group with abnormal movements? Do all the hamsters give an impression

of health (see Checklist, page 54)? If even one of the animals in the group acts peculiar, you should not buy any of them. The danger of infection is too great. On the other hand, if all the animals appear to be healthy, pick out the hamster you like best. Then you will have the job of choosing.

Hamster Species and Breeds

By now, you should have asked the question about the hamster's species, whether golden hamster or dwarf hamster, before acquiring and equipping the hamster's home. Nevertheless, here are a few bits of advice: Golden hamsters become almost double the size of dwarf hamsters and thus are easier to observe and perhaps more impressive for

Wild-colored, short-haired golden hamsters exhibit **primordial behavior** and are less susceptible to disease than other breeds.

younger children. Golden hamsters absolutely must be kept singly, and in the beginning they may be somewhat timid and prone to bite. However, they let themselves be tamed and then become very trusting. With the dwarf hamsters, the *Phodopus* species—that is, the Djungarian dwarf hamster, Campbell's dwarf hamster, and Roborovski dwarf hamster—can be kept in pairs or more in a sufficiently large cage. Chinese striped hamsters, on the other hand, are so aggressive that they—like the golden hamsters—are best kept separated.

The question of color and breed is largely a matter of taste. Personally, I lean to the wild-colored, short-haired form. They still exhibit the typical hamster behaviors and are also less susceptible to illness. To my mind, they are therefore best for beginners.

Age at Purchase

If you do not want to take on an older hamster from an animal shelter, your hamster should, in light of the short life span, be as young as possible. Young animals become accustomed to a new environment more quickly. Young animals can be taken from their mothers after the age of four weeks and can then live alone. Four to six weeks is thus the ideal age to let the hamster move in. However, at least in the pet store, the seller often does not know how old the animals are. So how can you tell if a hamster is older than it may be said to be? The best way to see is in comparison with an adult hamster. At five weeks the young of the golden hamster weigh on average 19 oz (55 g) and are thus half as large as a full-grown animal. Young animals rest in groups, while older hamsters—if they are kept in one cage in a pet store, for instance—are quarrelsome, rest alone, and often have violent conflicts with the fellow members of their species.

Male or Female?

There is hardly any difference in behavior between male and female hamsters. Male hamsters, especially golden hamsters, are somewhat more active, while

Satin hamsters are very popular as pets because of their silky soft coats.

▼

the activity of the female fluctuates during her four-day cycle. As a result of this cycle, females, if they are ready to breed, excrete some mucus from the genital opening, which can smell slightly unpleasant to sensitive noses. If you want to keep dwarf hamsters of the same sex together, be aware that the females are often less compatible with each other than males are.

transport the animal for long distances in this box, for instance in the car, without having to inspect it constantly. Should a longer car trip be necessary, then do not put the box with the hamster in it in the trunk; instead, place it on one of the seats and fasten a seatbelt around it. Use the heat and/or air conditioner in your car to regulate the tem-

DID YOU KNOW THAT . . .

. . . a new environment stresses the hamster?

There are test data on how the hamster feels if it is transferred from its usual cage into another. The heart rate of a golden hamster in this situation was measured with a small transmitter placed in its abdomen. The result was clear. Its heart rate rose by 150 beats per minute and it took more than half an hour before it returned to normal again. So, a change in scenery is pure stress for your little pet.

Transport Home

The pet store has plastic carrier boxes, which I recommend completely. This one-time investment quickly pays off. If you have to take the hamster to the veterinarian or you have discovered you have a general interest in small rodents, you will reach for this box over and over. The box should have a side length of at least 10 in. (25 cm) and be transparent. It will be closed with a perforated cover, which usually contains a little trapdoor through which the animal can be comfortably placed inside. You can

perature. The hamster can easily be harmed by extreme temperatures in winter and especially in summer. In the blazing sun, the air in the car heats up quickly, to which the animal's metabolism is very sensitive; hamsters cannot sweat or get rid of this warmth in any other way. Have the box filled with some of the litter from the hamster's cage at the pet store or the breeder's. Smell is the small animal's most sensitive sense. Hamsters become stressed when, in addition to the unusual environment, the smell of its litter changes.

Do not put a drinking bottle in the box either during the move or when taking long journeys. It will only leak when shaken. It is best to leave half an apple in the box for the hamster. It will be well provided with both food and moisture.

In the pet store the hamsters are usually "packed" into folding boxes for transport. Only take the animal home this way in an emergency. Aside from the closeness of this "home" and the missing litter, it will be easy for a hamster to free itself from this carton. Place this box unsupervised in your car, and it won't take long before the hamster has gnawed its way through the cardboard.

Then finding it again in or beneath the upholstery of the car will most likely require taking the seats apart entirely. So it is best to keep the carton in your hands (or in the hands of a passenger). Also do not forget to have the dealer give you a little bag with some litter from the sales cage.

And in case you do not have a carrying box, a plastic box with closed side walls are also suitable for transporting the animal. Since these containers do not have covers, however, they should be at least 12 in. (30 cm) deep. Naturally you should not let these alternative transport containers out of your sight.

CHECKLIST

First Health Check

- The hamster is lively, moves normally, and is constantly exploring its cage.

- It has a gently rounded body shape.

- There are no noticeable swellings or lumps to be seen on its body.

- Its fur is glossy.

- Its skin surface is unbroken.

- Its eyes are open, clear, shining, not sunken, and not protruding way out.

- The area around its anus is dry.

- Its nose is dry, and its ears are clean and uninjured.

The Hamster Moves In

The first hours and days are central as to whether your hamster will quickly learn to trust you. If you make no mistakes in introducing it to its new home, nothing more will stand in the way of a harmonious relationship.

The transport was enormously stressful for the hamster, so much so that now the first rule should be to do everything with a great deal of calm and patience.

The Hamster in Its New Home

Step 1: The first thing is to put two to three handfuls of litter from the old home into the ready and waiting new sleeping house. Food dish and water bottle should already be filled.

Step 2: Now carefully place the hamster in the cage. If you have transported it in the paper carton, place the carton with the hamster in the cage and carefully open the side so that the hamster can come out on its own.

Step 3: Now you must be patient. It would be best for the hamster if you left the room now. But on the other hand, it is one of the most satisfying moments to observe how your new pet takes possession of its new territory. Close the cage quickly and sit very quietly in front of it, not moving at all if possible and not making a sound.

Step 4: The hamster will probably take cover in its little house at first. Please be patient and avoid any changes in or at the cage.

Step 5: Aside from providing food and changing the drinking water, everything should proceed this way for a week. Under no circumstances should you look inside the sleeping house or lift it! At some point, the hamster will come out by itself and gradually begin to explore its new surroundings. It will take in the new scents and mark its territory with its own scent. If you have provided the cage with plenty of activity material, it will gradually take possession of all of it (see page 95). Even if you can hardly bear to wait until the hamster finally climbs onto its new exercise wheel, please don't push it in any direction. Any form of compulsion makes the small pet shy and anxious.

Step 6: When, after a few days, the hamster no longer runs anxiously around the cage, rests in its little house in the daytime, and begins its activities with thorough stretching and yawning, it has finally come to terms with its new home. Now you can cautiously begin to win the animal's trust.

Making Friends with the Hamster

Once the hamster has become used to its new environment, it is time to make friends. If you practice a little patience

Never try to force the hamster to do anything, or the first **tender bonds** of trust will be dissolved immediately.

and some skill, your little housemate will soon become used to your hand.

Step 1: The best friendships begin with small treats, which you offer the hamster in your hand. Feed it through the bars of the cage at first. For example, patiently hold out a little piece of apple, a peanut, or a mealworm until it eats out of your hand without any shyness. It is helpful if you rub your fingers beforehand with some litter from the cage so they have a familiar scent. After the hamster has become used to this type of feeding, go a step further.

Step 2: Open the cage. Lay your open hand, with food placed on it, in the cage. Sometime, maybe very quickly, but perhaps more slowly, the hamster will climb onto your hand and claim its reward. It is important that you remain relaxed and quiet the entire time and not force the hamster into anything.

Step 3: Once it is a matter of course for the little pet to get its food from your hand, you can try to stroke it gently with one finger at the back of the neck. If it runs away, try it again the next time. At some point the animal will perceive it as pleasant. Now let it climb from one hand to the other. Lift one hand slightly higher so that it has to make an effort to overcome the hurdle. If it enjoys that, you can congratulate yourself. You have done it, the hamster is hand tame!

The Right Way to Pick Up and Carry a Hamster

For a hamster that isn't used to the hand, being grasped and lifted up can cause great stress. So only take hold of the little pet when it is absolutely necessary—in the beginning, only for cleaning the cage. Proceed as cautiously as possible. There are different ways of picking the animal up and gently carrying it.

The container method

The best way is to work a little trick. You need a container for it, a big glass or a cardboard box. Again, rub the container with some litter, as extensively as possible. Place it in the cage or hold it in your hand close to the animal. Dwarf hamsters, in particular, are thus encouraged to take shelter inside. When the hamster creeps in, close the container with the other hand. Now you can

---

TIP

No surprise presents!

Never surprise anyone with a hamster for a present. When taking on an animal's care, a person assumes a responsibility that requires a certain amount of preparation and inner adjustment. Aside from the fact that the recipient might not like hamsters, you don't know if he or she has the time to devote to the animal's care.

gently carry it. This is a very protective measure and is especially recommended when the hamster is not tame yet!

Lifting with your hand

If the hamster is used to your hand, you can carry it in your hands. Never use gloves. With gloves, especially if they are leather ones, you do not have proper feeling, and either you grasp too loosely so that the hamster can fall to the floor or hold it too firmly, which can injure it. If your charge is still apt to bite, you had better use the container method. Using both hands, grasp the hamster from behind and form a sort of protective cave over it. Then push both hands together beneath the hamster and take it out of the cage. Be careful that it doesn't jump out of your hands as you do it. If the cage is too narrow or you have to take the animal out of a narrow niche, you can also grasp it from behind with one hand, thumb and forefinger placed behind the front legs, and push the other hand underneath the animal. **Note:** At this point I should point out that the hamster can be fatally injured if it is allowed to fall. A fall or jump from even table height can result in fatal spinal injuries. If ever—despite all precautions—the hamster bites one of your fingers, never—in the first shock—fling it away from you. Keep calm and place the hamster on a firm surface, such as the cage floor. As a rule it will then let go of your finger.

The neck hold

This type of lifting requires a great deal of practice and should therefore be left to professional breeders or the veterinarian.

In the neck grip, the hamster is grasped by a fold at the back of the neck. This rather warlike technique corresponds to the biology of the hamster, since it was seized in its mother's mouth this way as a young animal. It then falls into a slack posture and allows itself to be carried without resistance. Adult hamsters, however, generally have a very loose skin and can almost turn around inside it. To do the neck grip, approach the hamster from behind, place a hand on its back, and grasp the skin at the nape of the neck with thumb and forefinger.

This is the right way to carry a hamster. The hands form a protective cave around the animal.

New, unfamiliar items must be thoroughly examined from the start.

If you don't get enough skin in the hold, the hamster can turn around and bite. This method is most recommended for the *Phodophus* dwarf hamsters; otherwise, it is better not to use the neck grip on your hamster.

Note: Never try suddenly grabbing the hamster from above. It will feel that it is being seized by a predatory bird and, in response, will instantly roll onto its back and try to defend itself by biting.

MY HAMSTER

How curious is your hamster?

When your hamster has moved in with you, you can observe how it explores its new surroundings. Notice which objects it accepts immediately, which ones it just slowly works its way toward, and which ones are avoided completely.

The test begins:

Make a list of the items of equipment and note under each of them how often and how long the item is used by your hamster. What is most often used in the first few days and what utensils are, as it were, "put aside"? Thus you can quickly find out whether your hamster is quiet or is playful and what equipment proves to be especially hamster-friendly.

My test results:

Questions About Behavior and Adjustment

? How can I ease the adjustment period for my newly acquired hamster?

First, try to create as little stress to the hamster as possible even during the transport. Invest in a carrying box (see page 53) and put a little litter from the sales cage into the new box. When you get home, put the litter into the hamster home and, if possible, allow the hamster to run into the cage on its own. During the first week, try to work at or in the cage as little as possible. Only begin to make friends with your hamster after that (see page 55).

? What are medium hamsters?

There are about 20 hamster species extant in the world, which by the way are only found in the wild in Europe and Asia. They can be roughly divided into three groups according to their size: large, medium, and dwarf hamsters. The large hamsters comprise only one species, occurring in Europe, the wild field hamster (*Cricetus cricetus*). The medium hamster (Mesocricetus) includes four species: the Syrian golden hamster, the Turkish hamster, the black-chested hamster, and the Rumanian hamster. The remaining hamsters are dwarf hamsters. Among these are the four other species that are discussed in this book besides the golden hamster.

? Can dwarf hamsters be kept in groups?

The answer is an unequivocal "yes and no"! While golden hamsters must always be housed singly, you can try to keep dwarf hamsters of the genus *Phodopus*—that is, Campell's dwarf hamster, Djungarian dwarf hamster, and Roborovski dwarf hamster—in pairs or in small groups. Prerequisites, however, are a sufficiently large cage (at least 16 × 32 in. [40 × 80 cm] floor area) and the animals' familiarity with each other. They should have grown up together and otherwise should only be put together with the greatest caution. Keep your eye on the animals at all times. If conflicts occur, separate the hamsters immediately.

? Should my hamster be seen by a veterinarian immediately after purchase?

No, ordinarily this is not necessary. The hamster does not even receive any immunization shots. Surely you have already noted the advice on the appearance of a healthy hamster and have chosen your animal accordingly. You should only visit a veterinarian if your new pet shows some unexpected change in the course of acclimation.

My hamster only sits in its little house and grinds its teeth when I approach. Is this normal?

As a rule, yes, it is normal. The transport and the new environment mean big stress for the animal. So in this first period it takes every opportunity to withdraw. You should leave the hamster alone. The teeth grinding is a threatening behavior with which it reacts to disturbances.

My hamster bites if I take hold of it or try to catch it. What can I do?

Probably your hamster is not yet used to you or is not tame yet. The taming is a boring procedure that demands a great deal of patience. Your hamster still regards you as an enemy or an intruder into its territory, which must be fought. Therefore you must gradually earn the hamster's trust. If you need to catch the hamster to, say, clean its cage, use a large plastic or glass container and allow your new pet to crawl into it (see page 56). When a formerly tame hamster suddenly begins to bite, it can indicate an illness or injury. Your best bet is to go to the veterinarian.

Are there differences in behavior among the various breeds of the golden hamster?

It has been reported that teddy bear hamsters are peaceful; wild-colored hamsters are very active; and hamsters with other specific patterns or color variations are quarrelsome and hard to tame. Unfortunately there are no definitive studies about this. These reports are stories from individual hamster keepers, and to some degree they contradict each other. The truth is most likely that the animals are similar in behavior and are all tamed equally easily if one proceeds with the appropriate patience. I keep recommending the wild-colored hamsters, which are the favorites with seriously interested small-animal lovers.

Are cages with wire grills on the additional levels suitable for hamster keeping?

No, as advantageous as it is for the maintenance of the animal to have additional levels available in the cage, they must not be made of wire grating. Unless you cover the wire with sustainable material, the animals can fall between the bars as they are running over them and injure themselves. Thus it is better to use wooden floors. Have flat pieces of wood fastened to the existing wire grills. The best thing is to add small wooden ladders as edging and to put some litter on the floor. If the floors overlap and are connected with little ladders, your cage will come very close to optimal maintenance.

Good Food for Health and Fitness

When it comes to proper diet, hamsters are anything but undemanding. The small rodents need various kinds of grains as well as fruit, vegetables, and animal protein.

Dry Feed and Other Foods

In hamsters' native habitat, food is only abundant for about two months out of the year. So the animals stock up on food reserves. As pets they have food served to them, but they still hoard as much as they can.

Food in the Wild

Hamsters in their native habitat eat the leaves of certain plants, as well as their seeds or fruits. Especially in hot countries like Syria or southern Turkey, the growing season of plants is often only one to two months long. Then everything is dried up in the sun. Therefore the animals are very active during that time and hoard whatever they can to increase their food supply. Golden hamsters prefer to construct their burrows in fields so that they have their food right on their doorstep. Carefully checking in all directions, they come out of their burrows at twilight and run a few yards to the tastiest and juiciest plants. They especially like fields with legumes like lentils or chick peas. In a flash, their cheek pockets are stuffed full and then they whisk back into the protection of their burrows. Such "shopping trips" last only a few minutes. When it has grown completely dark, the golden hamsters stay in their burrow. They are thus protected from nocturnal predators such as foxes or owls. Besides vegetable food, golden hamsters and Campbell's and Djungarian dwarf hamsters, especially, also eat various insects and other invertebrate animals. They need this animal protein to prepare them for the lean times. During reproduction, in particular, animal protein is almost essential for the female.

Problem-free Feeding

Food for hamsters can be divided into three different groups. The main part of their diet consists of dry food with a grain base (feed mixtures). About 40 percent of the total amount of feed should consist of fresh food; the remainder is made up of animal protein snacks.

Fresh wild fruits like these rose hips are usually gladly received by all hamsters. ▶

Vegetable dry feed

Various dry feed mixtures for small rodents are available commercially and for the most part you can choose them without any concern. The basis of the mixture consists of seeds of different kinds of grains, rolled oats, and sunflower seeds, along with specially formulated feed flakes. Lab blocks are also

age. The following data are approximate values that should help you choose:

▸ Carbohydrates (main nutrients): 65 percent
▸ Raw protein (indicates protein content in the feed): 15–20 percent
▸ Raw fat (as little as possible): up to 5 percent
▸ Raw fiber (roughage, important for digestion): 8–10 percent
▸ Raw ash (minerals and trace elements): about 4 percent

DID YOU KNOW THAT . . .

. . . sweets obstruct the cheek pockets?

Hamsters definitely like sweet things. But you are not doing your small pet any good providing them. The hamster's cheek pockets become clogged by the sugar and then it can no longer eat. If this is not noticed in time, the hamster dies an unpleasant death from hunger. Therefore you should only spoil your little pet with healthy treats, such as a little piece of apple or banana.

available as nutritious hamster food. However, there are differences among food mixtures. Be especially careful that the mixtures do not contain sugar. Diseases of the gastrointestinal tract, and also diabetes, are attributable to too much sugar in the diet. Furthermore, the fat content of the food should not be too high. Sunflower kernels or nuts are known to contribute a lot of fat. Good hamster feed also contains a certain portion of animal protein, which can be added in various forms, such as dried meat or dried insects. Details of the nutrients are printed on the pack-

There is also the possibility of mixing the feed yourself, but besides the time needed, it requires great experience to find the right ingredients. You can safely try out different feed mixtures and then quickly discover your little pet's preferences. Besides, a variety-filled diet prevents deficiencies.

Quantity of food: Here there are varying recommendations, ranging on average from two to three teaspoons of food mixture per day. But since it is difficult to measure out precisely the amount necessary for your hamster, I urge you to make sure there is always some grain

Whether golden or dwarf hamsters, they all need a
balanced diet. To produce this yourself
requires a great deal of knowledge as to the right composition.

mixture in the hamster's feeding dish. However, you should check to see that the hamster is living up to its reputation and piling up food in a food corner or in the sleeping house. The house with a removable or flip-top roof helps you to inspect your hamster's stores (see page 43). Observe, too, whether the hamster takes certain foods out of the dish first according to its preference. For instance, in my experience those foods will be nuts or sunflower kernels, which, as already explained, are rich in fats. If you always refill with the same feed, your hamster will specialize in these treats and your well-thought-out mixture will not be effective. Therefore, pay careful attention that your hamster does not eat too much of the fatty diet. Another alternative is to purchase lab blocks from your pet supply store. Lab blocks prevent the hamster from picking out a specific food because your hamster will normally eat the whole thing.

Storage of food: When you buy food, make sure that the "use by" date has not expired. Do not buy too much food in advance, in spite of special offers, because you do not want to store it for too long. It's best to use an airtight closable jar for keeping food. These have the advantage of keeping out the dried-fruit moths. These moths always manage to lay their eggs in hard-to-get-at foodstuffs so that the eggs will hatch. Throw away affected feed and, of course, stored mixtures. Moth eggs are most likely to be found in feed mixtures that are sold from open containers. The larvae are only waiting until you get home to hatch. Buying such loose feed mixtures is therefore not recommended; the ingredients are also often unknown and, as a result, questionable. A problem with long storage is the frequently invisible development of mold in the feed. Small rodents are especially sensitive to these microorganisms and become ill when they consume this feed. Dampness and warm storage promote growth of these molds in the feed.

Hay is indispensable

Sufficient roughage in the food is an important aspect of a hamster's nutrition; therefore, see to it that your ham-

Feeding from your hand builds trust, especially when it tastes so good.

Healthy Treats

▶ **1** **Dried herbs or hay** provide roughage and prevent diarrheal illnesses. The movable ball ensures that the feed has to be worked for.

▶ **2** **Fresh plants** are gladly accepted. However, not all greens are good for the hamster (see Food List, below)

▶ **3** **Grapes** are tasty but relatively high in sugar. Therefore you should not offer them to your hamster very often.

ster always has enough hay available. Diarrheal illness, in particular, can be prevented with the proper amount of roughage.

Make sure that the hay is not mown at the edge of the street or in similar places exposed to exhaust fumes or pesticides. The hay should give the impression of freshness. If a high proportion of it is already breaking into little pieces, you should not buy it. On the other hand, it is a good sign if there are many meadow weeds in the hay along with the grass because these can supply important minerals. So buy hay that indicates portions of these on the label. Sometimes you can buy hay varieties with various greens already added. Besides, there are also dried greens available separately, which you should occasionally mix into the hay mixture for your small pet. You can gather greens yourself or dig them up in the garden and dry them in the protection of shade. Plants recommended for food are clover, alfalfa, mint, dandelion, net-

tle, chamomile, lemon or sweet balm, parsley, and other garden herbs, especially coneflower (Echinacea). But make sure these plants aren't sprayed with pesticides. If your hamster does not like aromatic greens, find out what herbs taste good to your little pet.

The Food List

Here you will find a listing of the foods you should offer your hamster all the time, just a little, or not at all.

Anytime

Dry plant foods: buckwheat, corn flakes (sugar-free), pea flakes, wheat grains, dried vegetables, grass seed, rolled oats, hemp seeds, hard bread, hay or dried herbs, millet seed, carob bean, chick peas, crispbread, foxtail millet, grain for bird seed, corn (also fresh corn ears), rice, panicle millet, sunflower kernels.

Fruits, vegetables, and herbs: apples, berries, pears, home-grown sprouts,

strawberries, fresh chick pea or lentil plants, daisies, cucumber, rose hips, shepherd's purse, couch grass, pumpkin, dandelion, carrots (no leaves!), parsley (not for pregnant females!), red beets, soy sprouts, watermelons, plantain, zucchini.
Protein and live foods: cottage cheese or natural yogurt, dried shrimp, dry dog or cat food, water fleas (*Gammarus*), egg whites, all insects, especially crickets, house crickets, grasshoppers, meal beetles, moths.
Branches: apple, pear, hazel, willow, poplar.

Rare snacks

"Hamster waffles," peanuts, hazel nuts, dog biscuits, pumpkin seeds, noodles (raw or cooked), raisins (unsulfured), walnuts, zwieback.
Fruits, vegetables, and greens: all kinds of lettuce, avocado, banana, nettle, blackberries, chicory, boiled potato, blueberries, raspberries, currants, kiwi,

clover (not for pregnant females!), tomato (no leaves!).
Protein and live foods: canned dog and cat food, plain cheese, mealworms, beef and chicken.
Branches: maple, linden, birch.

Under no circumstances

All sweets, bonbons, drops (also known as yogurt drops), acorns, salted nuts, spicy baked goods, gummy bears, chest-

---

TIP

High-voltage treats

Buy food without fatty nuts and sunflower seeds. Offer these as snacks only, and in between meals. A hamster should not eat more than one to two sunflower seeds or a half of a peanut or hazelnut or a quarter of a walnut per day. For dwarf hamsters, half of these amounts will be enough.

nuts, salt sticks, chocolate, baked goods containing sugar.
Fruits, vegetables, and greens: all cabbage vegetables, pineapple, cow parsnip/hogweed/pigweed, beans, ivy, poisonous plants, cress, carrot leaves, peach, apricot, nectarine, raw potato, spinach, stone fruits, tomato leaves, citrus fruits, onions and all members of the allium family.

Protein and live food: pork, egg yolk.
Branches: houseplants, horse chestnut, oak, evergreens, cherry, plum.

FEEDING PLAN FOR YOUR HAMSTER

FOOD AND QUANTITY

Daily	Two teaspoons of food mixture with grain base Some fresh food (e.g., pieces of apple, little pieces of grapes, a tiny little piece of cucumber or carrot, two to three dandelion leaves).
Every two or three days	A mealworm or a cricket A raisin or a nut Some hard bread or roll Possibly replenish water
Weekly	Two to three branches for gnawing (e.g., beech, hazelnut, willow, poplar, apple, pear) A piece of foxtail millet twice A teaspoon of cottage cheese or fresh cheese A teaspoon of dry dog or cat food Wash water bottle

Moist Food Provides Strength

Fresh and live food are just as important for your hamster as dried food. Gnawing materials such as fresh branches contain valuable minerals among other things. But above all, they ensure that the hamster can sharpen its teeth.

Fruits and vegetables as well as green plants contain vitamins and minerals that are important for the nutrition of your hamster. Therefore you should offer fresh food regularly.

Provide Fresh Food — But How?

It is possible to provide fresh carrots, apples, or cucumbers without any difficulty (see The Food List, page 66). When buying fresh food, make sure that it has not been chemically treated. If you want to be quite certain, buy fresh food in a health food store.

It is very important to give the hamster only small quantities. Fresh food spoils easily and rotten food can make the hamster sick. Besides, improper feeding with fresh vegetables often triggers diarrheal diseases. Instead, begin with small pieces of apple, carrot, or cucumber, or try some iceberg lettuce. Offer the hamster the fresh food in the evening. The next day search the cage thoroughly for remnants of food, including the sleeping house and other hiding places. After all, there has doubtless been a hoarder at work again.

Your hamster will be especially pleased with freshly-picked dandelion leaves. Two to three leaves per feeding are enough. Please make sure to check for truly fresh plants where you are collecting feed. You should thus avoid the edges of much-traveled roads, which are often sought out by cats and dogs. If you have your own yard, you are naturally on the safe side. Here is one more piece of advice: Don't put any fresh food on the hamster's wooden sleep house. The damp feed promotes the development of mold in the wood.

Note: The hamster gains a large portion of its liquid requirement from the fresh food, so you need not wonder if the drinking bottle is untouched. On the other hand, caution is required here, too. Always monitor the water level in the drinking bottle! Some hamsters continue to drink out of habit, despite

TIP

Remove food remains

Spoiled remains of juicy food like fruit and vegetables must be removed regularly from the sleeping house. Your hamster will get sick otherwise. A house with a fold-back roof facilitates inspection without disturbing the arrangement your animal has made of the individual kinds of food.

Has Your Child Lost Interest in the Hamster?

"Our 11-year-old son no longer takes pleasure in looking after his hamster, Romeo. What can we do now without having to give the animal away to a shelter?"

Even if you have carefully prepared your son for keeping a hamster, it can happen that a child loses interest in his animal over time and perhaps neglects it. First, you should examine yourself in that case: Have you always shown interest in the hamster? Have you been engaged when your child has talked about his hamster, its behavior, his advances in establishing trust, or his problems with the animal?

Stimulating interest

If you have always maintained an interest in the hamster but nevertheless your child no longer wants to care for the hamster, your psychological skills are needed now. Explain to your child once again what the consequences for the hamster will be if it is no longer properly cared for. Also explain sympathetically that hamsters, especially, are very place-centered and that it is not good for the animal to be passed on like a toy. Let your child think this over and listen to the arguments. Advise patience if the hamster has not become tame as quickly as your child perhaps expected. Try to point out new aspects of the animal's behavior. Perhaps you can try out one of the My Pet Tests with the child to possibly awaken new interest. For example, you could discover together what preferences the little hamster has (see What Tastes Best to Your Hamster, page 72) or what time it really becomes active (see page 42). Help your child find the best way to make room for hamster care. Perhaps you must sometimes help take care of his hamster, but then please, only in such a way that your child feels he maintains "oversight" over the care despite your help.

If none of this helps

Of course, it is possible that in spite of everything, the child cannot form any attachment to the animal, that perhaps he may have even been bitten. In this case, do not use pressure. It would be detrimental to both parties—animal and human—and no solution in the long run. There are only a few options: Either you, the parent, can take over the care of the animal, or you must try to find another caregiver for the hamster. If neither option works, then the only course left is to take the animal to a shelter.

abundantly available fresh food. This can lead to diseases of the digestive system. Better to detach the water bottle if you are regularly feeding fresh food. Dwarf hamsters, in particular, get along well without water bottles.

Gnawing Material

Hamsters have rootless chisel teeth, which grow constantly and must be worn down. Therefore the hamster always needs gnawing material. Place some branches and twigs of fruit wood like apple, pear, or cherry in the cage (see The Food List, page 66) for it. The branches need not be leafless or, in spring, the flowers need not be removed either. Then, however, you should keep inspecting the hamster's stores to be sure they have not developed any mold. Obviously it is important when collecting branches yourself to be sure that the trees have not been sprayed.

Protein and Live Food

As already mentioned, hamsters in the wild are not purely vegetarian but need a good proportion of animal protein in their diets to thrive. Hamsters kept as pets are no different. Although protein-containing elements are already included in some food mixtures, as a rule the amount is not enough for an optimal supply. So you should give your little rodent an extra portion of protein two or three times per week. For this you can try to imitate natural conditions and feed live food. But if you have any problem with that, you can also fulfill the protein requirement with cottage cheese, fresh cheese, chopped beef, or dog food. Feed only as much as the hamster takes in right away. Offer the protein in a separate dish and remove it when the hamster no longer eats from it. It is even better to combine the feeding of tasty treats with building a relationship with your pet, for the small pet is very interested in its food. Offer it

One can certainly exert oneself a little for a delicious strawberry. Hiding food provides variety in the hamster's daily life.

MY HAMSTER

What tastes best to your hamster?

Find out what your hamster's favorite food is. If you construct a course in the room or in the cage, you can also test your pet's sense of smell.

The test begins:
Hide a few treats either in the cage or in the room in places that are difficult to get to. Then observe whether your hamster energetically seeks out the food sources. If not, the food was probably not very tempting. Try it again with something different. If you then have discovered your hamster's favorite food, you can time how long it takes for it to "scour" the entire course.

My test results:

some cottage cheese or some live food at first with a little wooden stick and then on the tip of a finger. Wait until it has licked it off. Offer mealworms, for example, for live food. These are not actually worms, but the larvae of the black meal beetle (*Tenebrio molitor*).

Raising mealworms

Mealworms can be kept or even raised very easily.
How it is done: It is best to use a lidded plastic dish about 4 in. (10 cm) deep, which you provide with small air holes. On the bottom of the dish spread a layer of rolled oats about ¼ in. (1 cm) deep. You can also use stale bread or rolls instead of oats. Buy 3.5 oz (100 g) of mealworms at the pet store and place

them in the dish. The larvae do not need moisture so finish up by putting about four layers of folded newspaper on top. Now you can leave the whole thing alone for four weeks, and then maybe add more rolled oats or bread. The worms crawl in between the sheets of newspaper, so they can be easily picked out. The pupae that form after a while also taste good to the hamster, as do, of course, the hatching black meal beetles. Once the beetles have hatched, however, you must be especially careful to keep the breeding container tightly closed. The beetles are very active and can fly.
Feeding: The larvae are easy to grab with tweezers or can be picked up with two fingers (trust yourself!).

However, moderation is advised, since the mealworms are very fatty. You should not offer your little friend more than three to four worms a week.

Buying live food

Somewhat larger and thus fattier than mealworms are the larvae of the large ground beetle (*Zoophobas morio*), which you can sometimes buy in pet stores and feed sparingly to the hamster. However, the highlight is the feeding of crickets or grasshoppers. These are also sold alive in good pet stores. Keeping them is not as easy as keeping the mealworms, however, so do not buy too many at a time. Usually the insects of various sizes are sold in small plastic containers; here the larvae look very similar to the full-grown insects and can be differentiated from them mainly by size. At home it is difficult to feed the individual insects without having them escape, hide behind your bookcase, and drive you crazy for weeks on end with their "singing." One solution is the cricket keeper, which can keep up to 30 crickets at a time. Another method is to place the cricket container in a large bucket and to only open the container there. Then remove a single cricket with the tweezers and place it in a tall glass. Shake the crickets, one at a time, out of the glass into the hamster cage. You will no longer recognize your little pet! The dwarf hamsters, in particular, become astonishingly active when it is a matter of capturing the cricket.

Crickets are a special treat. It is a real joy to watch your pet dash through the cage in pursuit of its elusive prey.

Small Rewards for Between Times

Naturally you would like to make your little pet happy and spoil it now and again with something very special. The industry has recognized this and therefore offers all kinds of snacks for hamsters. As hard as it may be for you—not the least because of the colorful packages decorated with the obviously happy hamster—keep away from them! These snacks mostly contain sugar and are not suitable for your hamster. The

Feed mealworms sparingly and one at a time. That way you have good control over the quantity.

attractive reward will actually shorten its life. The hamster can get diabetes or have other metabolic disturbances. Do not even begin to get young hamsters used to them.

Healthy treats: So what nice thing can you do for your pet? In principle, mealworms, crickets, or some cottage cheese or fresh cheese, offered on a finger, are already fantastic snacks. The nibbling sticks offered commercially are also worth considering, if they do not contain sugar or honey additives. Occasionally you can reward the hamster with a raisin. It is also possible to see if the hamster likes little pieces of dry dog or cat food. If you like to bake, you might try making some "extra tidbits" for your hamster without the added sugar. Instead, use ingredients with whole-wheat flour, rolled oats, sesame seeds, and grated carrots (see The Food List, page 66).

Salt or Mineral Lick Stone?

Should you hang a salt lick stone in the cage? Here the opinions diverge quite a lot. The fact is that many hamster breeders have kept and bred hundreds of hamsters without ever offering them a salt or mineral lick. If the animals are fed a varied diet, they do not need these additional sources of cooking salt or minerals. On the contrary, very high salt intake can burden the kidneys unnecessarily. Usually the animals leave the hanging stone completely untouched anyway. The same holds true for a mineral—or limestone—in principle. However, the extra intake of calcium is not quite so problematic. So, again, a hamster fed a normal and varied diet does not need any stones in the cage.

Vitamin Supplements?

If you follow the advice for a healthy diet, the hamster needs no additional vitamins. You can safely reject enriched drinking water or the offers of a "vitamin drink for hamsters." Here, too, vitamins can hurt rather than help your animal. Vitamin C is an acid and can acidify the urine when there is too much of it. Too much vitamin D leads to metabolic disturbances.

Food Plants
at a Glance

Suitable plants

You can offer your hamster these foods anytime: apple, cucumber, strawberries, daisies, rose hips, shepherd's purse, dandelion, carrots, plantain, parsley, and soy sprouts.

◀ Clover

You should only give your hamster this food plant occasionally (see The Food List, page 66). Clover can lead to considerable problems, especially for females during pregnancy.

◀ Rose hips

For most hamsters fresh rose hips (free of chemical spraying) are a marvelous feast. They are a healthy treat like sunflower seeds, which you can offer your pet in the right quantities without a second thought.

Not too often

You should not feed these fresh foods too often: lettuce, avocado, banana, nettle, chicory, boiled potato, blackberries, raspberries, currants, blueberries, kiwi, and tomato.

◀ Dandelion

All hamsters love fresh dandelion leaves and it is easy to provide. However, please do not ever collect dandelion from the edge of a road. The plants there are too heavily loaded with toxic auto emissions.

Well-cared For and Totally Healthy

Hygiene is an important basic requirement for your hamster to remain healthy. Just don't overdo it—the little pet does not like to be constantly disturbed.

Proper Care Prevents Illness

Hamsters are relatively easy to take care of, compared to other pets. However, this only applies to animals that are properly maintained. This means that you must provide your pet with a large cage, a healthy diet, a constant supply of gnawing material, free runs, and activities.

I have observed hamsters in their natural habitat and experienced how sensitively they respond to disturbances. We wanted to see the activity of the golden hamster in the evening and morning hours. Motionless, we waited patiently some 33 feet (10 m) away from the burrow for a little head to pop out of the hole eventually. Despite the greatest caution on our part, the burrow was abandoned that next day because something had apparently seemed suspicious to the hamster.

Care Can Cause Stress

This story clearly demonstrates that hamsters do not like changes in their environment. Also as a pet, the little hamster remembers all the objects in its cage and their scent. If something is suddenly different from the way it was before, it acts uneasy and stressed. Therefore, you must try to find a compromise between as little disturbance as possible and the necessary hygiene. The following pages spell out what your contribution to the care of the hamster and its quarters should be.

Regular care measures

Daily: Inspect the hamster's food dish to see if it is filled with grain feed. Refill it if necessary. Also take a peek into the sleeping house. If the hamster has deposited seeds there, leave it exactly as it is. But check whether there are also the remains of fresh food inside. By all means, these should be removed. You should also look for remains of fresh food throughout the entire cage (see page 69). Try not to stress the hamster too much as you do it. For instance, be careful not to move all the toys and/or equipment. Check the water

A balanced diet is one of the most important requirements for the health of your hamster.

level in the drinking bottle and fill it with fresh water.

Twice a week: As already noted, the hamster chooses a corner of its cage as a bathroom, which you should clean every three days. If you have succeeded in placing a little litter pan in that spot and your hamster actually uses it, the pan must be cleaned. Otherwise remove

bottle brush). Fill it again with tap water.

Every three to four weeks: If your hamster is the lucky tenant of a large cage (see page 33), a thorough monthly cleaning is enough. Otherwise, you should develop a feeling for when this relatively time-consuming procedure, and one that is especially uncomfortable for your charge, is necessary. Excessive cleanliness is actually out of place, since the new arrangement of the cage

DID YOU
KNOW THAT . . .

. . . grooming is very important to hamsters?

Hamsters usually perform intensive grooming at the beginning of their activity cycle. A firmly established process of grooming is evident. Both front legs are raised over the head, one at a time or synchronized. The hind legs are also used. The grooming process is so firmly programmed that a changed order can be taken as an indication of illness.

the litter from the corner with a small scoop and replace it with new litter.

Note: Never use the commercial deodorizer sprays. The smell will only irritate the hamster.

Weekly: Remove all food from the dish and clean it thoroughly with hot water—without soap or detergent. If the food dish is very dirty, however, you can also put it in the dishwasher. The high temperature in the dishwasher helps to eliminate the detergent smell. Empty the water bottle, and as with the food dish, wash out the bottle with hot water and no detergent or soap (use a

takes a heavy toll on the hamster and can even shorten its life span. However, if the cage is small, it must be cleaned more often. Some hamsters deposit their urine throughout the cage. If this is the case, you must clean more often. Two cages connected with tubes can be cleaned alternately. If that is not possible, you must take the hamster out of the cage temporarily.

Where to put the hamster during housecleaning?

A carrying box comes in handy (see page 53) during housecleaning.

Hamsters can become stressed and will react very uneasily
to change. The cage arrangement
should be exactly the same after cleaning as before.

The animal can wait in the box for the
duration of the cleaning. Fill the box
beforehand with old litter from the cage
and maybe add a small cardboard box
so that the hamster has a place to hide.
Then carefully take the little rodent out
of its cage with a glass and place it in
the carrier box (see page 56). If you do
not have a carrier, another plastic box
will do. It must, however, have walls
that are at least 12 in. (30 cm) high. In a
pinch, you can also let the hamster wait
in a bucket that contains some old litter.

Housecleaning in the hamster cage

Equipment: Dry brush the sleep house
or items of equipment made of wood.
After some time or if they are badly
soiled, items made of wood should be
replaced. Clean plastic or clay items
with hot water and a brush.
Litter: Remove all litter and hoarded
food, but save some of the old litter.
Floor pan: Remove the floor pan and
clean it with hot water and a brush. If
the pan is very dirty, you can use a few
squirts of unscented dishwashing detergent in the water. You can remove stub-
born items like dried urine in the toilet
corner with vinegar; the use of a disin-
fectant is not necessary.
Cage: Use vinegar to clean the cage.
Wash down the bars with a dampened
cloth and rinse well. Let everything dry
thoroughly, and then put everything
back into the cage.

Refurnishing the cage

Put a fresh layer of litter in the floor
pan, but place some of the old litter on
top. Make sure that all the equipment
items are placed in their original locations. Maybe make a little sketch for
yourself beforehand as a reminder.
Finally, put some fresh food into the
cage. After you have reinstalled the
"master of the house," the hamster
needs a day of rest to reorient itself. It
will run around the cage excitedly and
will need to reestablish its personal
markings.

*The hamster can
stay in this carry-
ing box during the
cage cleaning.*

Hamster Care Made Easy

Except for a few care procedures that require your touch, the hamster sees to its own impeccable appearance.

Coat care

The basic care of the hamster's coat is firmly anchored in its program of behavior. You can observe this any evening at the beginning of its activity period. A healthy hamster stretches and yawns with mouth open wide. It begins with grooming its coat thoroughly, during which it cleans its little body with its back and front legs. This means that

Sand bath: Your hamster may enjoy a shallow dish of chinchilla sand (from the pet store) in the cage. Rolling in a sand bath can support your hamster's grooming significantly. But don't be disappointed if the hamster does not take much interest in the dish. Bathing in sand differs among individuals. Golden hamsters, especially, rarely use the sand bath.

Water bath: Never try to bathe the hamster in water! The little steppe dweller is not adapted for this at all. The fur dries very slowly and the hamster can easily catch cold after such a

Especially after waking and after meals the **coat** is brought to **high gloss**. Hamsters groom their fur very intensively and constantly.

with short-haired hamsters, you need not interfere. Problems only occur with the teddy bear hamsters. Their long fur can mat, especially in the anal area, or food particles can get stuck in it. It is better not to try to remove the remains with a comb or a brush. Experience shows that to be possible in only the rarest cases, especially since brushing tends to greatly limit the patience of your pet. The one thing that helps here is a pair of scissors. As a hamster hairdresser, you will have the best success with small, curving scissors. Don't worry about giving your pet a bad haircut. The hair grows back in a short time. Introduce your teddy bear hamster to the procedure when it is young. That way you will prevent infections of the anal area.

procedure. Besides, bathing interferes with the natural skin oils.

Claws

As a rule, the nails of the hamster should not be cut. The nails are worn down on their own through the animal's innate need to scratch. Nevertheless, you should inspect your pet every four weeks or so for nails that are too long. The veterinarian must cut overgrown nails!

Dental anomalies

Dental changes are not as frequent with hamsters as they are with, for example, guinea pigs. Besides, you should be placing branches in the cage regularly for the hamster to shorten its teeth on. If you are not always able to provide the

Thorough grooming is a must for a healthy hamster. In particular, the grooming ritual occurs after waking, emptying the cheek pockets, and at the end of meals.

◀ 1

With its two front paws, the hamster strokes its head and ears several times. Hamsters with short fur take care of grooming their coats on their own. Long-haired hamsters need your help.

2 ▶

With long-haired hamsters, grooming the coat is not sufficiently provided for in their genetic behavior program. This means that they cannot groom their abundant fur adequately on their own.

◀ 3

Cleaning the back legs is not so easy, but it must be done. Hamsters use not only their front feet but also their tongues for coat care.

4 ▶

right branches, just offer the hamster little pieces of wood or chew toys. Check the wood every now and then, since the hamster can incur injuries in this area. You should look out for congenital tooth misplacement when buying the animal (see page 54). If deformities occur, get the diagnosis of the veterinarian and leave the possible treatment to him or her.

With regular observation of your hamster's appearance and behavior, you will be able to recognize the signs of illness quickly.

Common Illnesses

Hamsters are not very susceptible to disease if they are properly cared for.
However, the little pets are especially sensitive to stress, wide fluctuations
of temperature, an unvaried diet or spoiled food, and poor cage hygiene.

 To some extent, hamsters are adapted to extreme living conditions and therefore have a well-developed immune system. So diseases in your pet are rather rare if it is properly cared for. Also, there are very few hamster-specific diseases. Inspect daily using the checklist to see if your hamster is healthy.

Signs of Illness

You should consult the veterinarian immediately if you notice any of the following signs:

Behavior: The animal is apathetic; is not active in the evenings; is aggressive and easily irritated; exhibits disturbed movements; limps; drags its body; does not eat; trembles; is frightened; scratches itself.

Body in general: Wet anal region; distended, hard and tight belly; weight loss of more than a quarter of an ounce (7 g) per week; diarrhea; discoloration on the legs; wasting; hunched posture; very long nails.

Fur or skin: Ruffled and ungroomed fur; swellings; wounds; fur loss; scabs.

Eyes: Tearing and red; protruding; sticky; half closed, or dry.

Nose and breathing: Nasal discharge; breath sounds; sneezing.

Mouth area: Heavy saliva secretion; scabs between the lips; cheek pockets visible in mouth; cheek pockets not completely emptied; tooth length or placement abnormal.

Visit to the Veterinarian

If you discover changes in your hamster, you should consult a veterinarian. Do not let too much time go by and do not try to carry out your own treatment ideas. Natural health methods can be accompanied by the expert treatment of a veterinarian if need be! Find out if there is a veterinarian in your area who is experienced in treating small animal diseases. If you do not find a specialist, do not be afraid to ask the veterinarian

TIP

Cage cleaning

The thorough cleaning of the cage should always take place during the hamster's activity period. Combine it with a free run for your little charge. The burden on the animal will thus be minimized. Make yourself a "cleaning calendar" in which you enter your cleaning measures.

of your choice whether he or she has ever treated hamsters. Possibly the veterinarian can refer you to a colleague. When you find a veterinarian, make sure that your pet is thoroughly examined and the treatment methods and their risks are carefully explained to you. Below are some of the most common illnesses of hamsters that you may encounter.

Mites or Fungus Attack

Symptoms: Does your hamster scratch itself often and run around in the cage restlessly? Does it have an unkempt coat or any fur loss in spots that reveal reddened and scabby skin?
Possible causes: Fur or mange mites. The exact diagnosis can only be rendered by microscopic examination of the parasites. You may be able to make the little spider mites visible by holding the hamster over a sheet of white paper and stroking its fur with a finger or, better, a comb. Because mite infestation usually indicates a diminished immune response in the animal, you should check the animal's maintenance conditions (too small a cage, dirty food or bad diet, stress). Also, excessive cleanliness can result in the hamster's being unable to develop any immunities.
Treatment: Under no circumstances should you try to get rid of the annoying parasites yourself with solutions or sprays on the body. Get the advice of a veterinarian promptly (see Zoonoses, page 90).

Diarrhea

Symptoms: Are the feces of your hamster gooey or even watery and is the anal region dirty? Is the animal not as active as before and is it also eating less?
Possible causes: Most often, the cause is a bacterial infection, such as *Salmonella*. Also, poisoning from eating toxic houseplants can indicate its presence with diarrhea. Have you recently changed its food or given an unusually large amount of fresh food? Or has the hamster eaten something lying on the floor during a free run?
Treatment: The first measure is to stop giving it any more fresh food and to clean its anal region in order to prevent inflammation. Then consult a veterinarian as soon as possible (within 24 hours).

Wet Tail

Symptoms: Does your hamster have damp spots in the tail region, as well as diarrhea?
Possible causes: Among other causes, colon bacteria are presumed to trigger

TIP

Know the signs of age

The little hamster no longer comes alertly out of its house in the evening—as it used to—but instead stays curled up inside. It hoards little food and moves uncertainly. Its fur grows unkempt, and it loses weight. Eventually the time will come when you'll find your pet at peace in the cage.

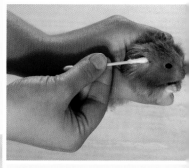

2 **Combing** the coat is an extremely uncomfortable procedure for the long-haired hamster. With a severely dirtied coat, it's better to cut off the fur.

1 **Properly immobilizing:** For giving medications, for instance, it is necessary to grasp the hamster just behind the front legs and immobilize it.

3 **Dirt can be removed** from the hamster's fur, as a rule, with the help of a damp cotton swab.

the disorder. The illness is provoked by high stress levels, especially in young hamsters. The disease frequently appears in young hamsters in the separation phase from the mother.

Treatment: As a first aid measure, stop giving your hamster any fresh food and clean the anal region in order to prevent inflammation. Then visit the veterinarian as soon as possible (within 24 hours).

Impaction or Prolapse of the Cheek Pockets

Symptoms: Does the hamster try unsuccessfully to stroke out its cheek pockets? Does it hesitate to eat?

Possible causes: The cheek pockets are impacted. He may have eaten sticky or fibrous substances (e.g., gummy bears, raisins, chocolate, dried fruit).

In a prolapse of the cheek pockets, one of the pockets can turn inside out with stroking and hang out of the mouth. Fortunately, this rarely occurs.

Treatment: In both instances, only the veterinarian can help. Impacted cheek pockets lead to serious infections and abscesses.

Colds

Symptoms: The symptoms are similar to those in humans. The animal sneezes, the nose can run, you hear a whistling sound when the hamster breathes.

Possible causes: Mistakes in maintenance are usually the cause of colds. Perhaps the hamster has been in a draft

The administration of medications works best **with the help of mealworms**. Cover one of them with the medication and hold it under the hamster's nose.

or subject to wide fluctuations of temperature.

Treatment: Present the animal to the veterinarian immediately. Perhaps he or she will prescribe antibiotics, which you should administer to your hamster according to directions. Under no circumstances should you give the animal antibiotics according to a regimen that is prescribed for humans. These medications are life-threatening for the hamster!

Otherwise you can promote healing by heating part of the cage with a heat lamp. Place the lamp far enough from the cage so that the temperature does not go higher than 86°F (30°C), even right under the lamp. The hamster must be able to escape the warmth.

Hamsters who stay in their house all the time may be sick.

Tumors

Symptoms: Have you discovered a hard spot or a bump under the hamster's skin when you were petting it?

Possible causes: It could be a matter of tissue proliferation. This illness is not attributable to the quality of care. It occurs spontaneously, especially in older animals.

Treatment: Discuss with your veterinarian whether the tumor can or must be removed by an operation. If the tumor is relatively small (about pea size), an operation will certainly remove it. If the hamster is older than 18 months and the tumor is already large, it is better to relieve the animal from its suffering.

Mouth and Nose Sores

Symptoms: Corners of the mouth, lips, and nose of the hamster are reddened or scabbed by progressive skin breakdown.

Possible causes: As a result of an unbalanced diet, tiny cracks will form in the skin, into which bacteria or fungus can settle.

Treatment: The veterinarian usually orders a salve. Pay attention to the vitamin nutrition of your pet!

Fractures

Symptoms: The hamster can no longer walk.

Possible causes: Most accidents occur during a free run in the house. The hamster jumps from a high edge, such as a table or chair. The small hamsters often cannot judge distance, owing to their limited vision, and jump from great heights. Caution is also required when you hold the hamster in your hand. Always secure it with a second hand because it will leap down from there, too.

Heat Shock

Symptoms: Your hamster lies apathetically on the floor and breathes very rapidly.
Cause: Hamsters have no sweat glands or other regulating mechanisms that protect them from heat. When temperatures rise in the wild, they retreat into

DID YOU KNOW THAT . . .

. . . these are not signs of illness?

In the male, especially in summer, the testicles descend from the abdomen for cooling. The black spots on the flanks of the hamster are scent glands, with which they mark their territory. Full cheek pockets need not be a sign of illness. Sometimes the hamster has simply not had a chance to empty them yet. Females have a yellowish secretion from the vagina every four days. (→ Estrus, page 110.)

Treatment: The extent of the injury can only be determined by X-ray at the veterinarian's office. Unfortunately, fractures in the extremities or injury to the spinal column are successfully treated only in rare instances. If this happens to your hamster, it is better to put the animal out of its misery. Occasionally smaller fractures (e.g., toes) can heal easily.

their burrows, where it is never warmer than 54°F (12°C). Temperatures higher than 77°F (25°C) should therefore be avoided. Especially during transport of the hamster in a car, the interior can quickly heat up in summer (see page 53). If it becomes too warm in the house, place a damp cloth over the cage. Another good method of cooling off is to lay a freezer block on top of the cage roof so that it cannot be nibbled on. If the hamster is kept in higher temperatures for an extended period of time or in the bright sun at all, its metabolism breaks down. When this

Saying Good-bye

"Our daughter's hamster is almost three years old. Sooner or later it is going to die. Our daughter is very attached to the animal. How shall we comfort her when it dies?"

Small rodents often have very short life spans. Golden hamsters can live to be four years old at most; dwarf hamsters, up to three years old. So you are right that the death of your daughter's golden hamster can occur shortly. Some parents are reluctant to give their child an animal with such a short life expectancy. But parents can instead see it as a chance to prepare the child for the fragile circle of life.

Giving consolation

One can refer to a two-year-old golden or dwarf hamster as being very advanced in age, and you should now begin to prepare your child for its death. If the hamster is seriously ill or has a larger injury, it is often better for the animal, after consultation with the veterinarian, to put it to sleep. Such a farewell is always painful for the child and perhaps also for you. You have become fond of the animal, since many events are connected with it. Now you face the difficult task of comforting your child. Explain to him or her that the animal will be released from its suffering and pain. Perhaps your child will understand that the development of new species must have as a precursor the death of the individual creature. So that hamsters, humans, and other living things can evolve, new variants must constantly arise and pass away again. The life expectancy of the hamster varies with individuals and depends on many factors, not on the maintenance conditions alone. Take comfort with your child that you have done everything for the animal up to this time of its life.

A grave site is important

Permit your child to bury his or her animal in the garden or another spot (see page 134). The grave site can be visited and cared for so that the tie to the animal can remain in existence for a while longer. Children often regard their animal as their dearest friend, with whom they can talk over everything and who understands them. It is a mistake to buy a new hamster immediately. This way the animal is perceived as a replaceable object, and your child receives a very misguided lesson as to the value of a fellow creature.

occurs, quickly move the animal to a cooler place and moisten the mouth area with water. You can also fan cool air onto the hamster or blow air with a hair dryer (with the heat turned off). When the hamster has recovered slightly, give it some water.

Eye Diseases

Symptoms: The hamster's eyes tear excessively; they protrude or are inflamed.
Possible causes: It can be a bacterial infection of the eyes. The trigger is often a slight injury to the eye, produced by inappropriate litter, for example, or by hay.
Treatment: Only the veterinarian can help! After a precise diagnosis, he or she will probably prescribe treatment with an eye salve.

Bites

Symptoms: Bite wounds usually occur in the anal or genital (testicle) areas or on the animal's flanks.
Cause: If, against all recommendations, hamsters are kept in groups or the females are not ready to mate, the animals can inflict bite wounds. Naturally the animals must be housed separately at once.
Treatment: While smaller wounds heal quickly within a few days, hamsters with large, bleeding wounds should be seen by a veterinarian.

Diabetes

Symptoms: The disease is not always easy to recognize. If your hamster is already older, has an increased body

A heat lamp can promote healing. However, it is essential to monitor the cage temperature so that the patient does not become overheated.

MY HAMSTER

How much does your hamster weigh?

The body weight is an important factor for the health of your pet. Check it on a weekly basis. For this you will need a kitchen scale. The most precise is a scale with a digital reading.

The test begins:

For weighing, use a plastic container in which you can place the hamster. Do not forget to subtract the weight of the container from the total weight. Create a table with the readings on it. What is the starting weight? How quickly does your hamster put on weight? Is the weight constant or does it fluctuate? If your hamster loses more than 0.25 oz (7 g) per week, you should consult a veterinarian.

My test results:

weight, produces a lot of urine, or has clouded eyes it could have diabetes.

Cause: The "sugar disease" can also affect hamsters. In most cases a diet containing too much sugar or too much fat is to blame.

Treatment: Of course only the veterinarian can establish the final diagnosis in this case. For prevention, you should always provide a well-balanced, healthy diet for your pet (see page 62). A regular feeding of rich treats only will harm your hamster.

Zoonoses

Zoonoses are animal diseases that can be transmitted to humans. Luckily this is rather rare in hamsters. Basically there are two possibilities to consider: fungus diseases and lymphocytic choriomeningitis (LCM).

The previously discussed fungus infections of hamsters, which are seen as fur loss or scab development, can also be transmitted to humans (see page 86). The veterinarian will take a scab sample from the spot (which is usually circular) and try to develop a fungus culture from it. Only then is a precise diagnosis possible. You must always disinfect your hands after contact with the animal. Inadequate nutrition, stress, and unclean maintenance of the hamster can cause fungus infections.

Lymphocytic Choriomeningitis (LCM)

Symptoms: The signs of illness are similar to those of a cold, with mucus membrane inflammation and disturbed general condition. In rare cases, tonic convulsions and paralysis are observed. This very rare disease of the central nervous system appears only in young hamsters up to three months old that have had contact with infected mice in animal-breeding mills. Older animals are not attacked by the disease. Symptoms in humans are fever, fatigue, and flu-like symptoms such as head, joint, and muscle ache. The fever can last up to two weeks. The disease usually advances without complications. However, there may also be a serious progressive form that can lead to meningitis. An infected pregnant woman can transmit the virus to the fetus, resulting in a miscarriage. In Germany, infections have occasionally occurred in humans in recent years. The chances for recovery in humans are quite good, and deaths are very rare. If you think that you have these flu-like symptoms after acquiring a young hamster in your household, you should consult your doctor. Tell him about the hamster care. Pregnant women should avoid contact with the hamster and avoid hamster-related cleaning tasks.

Cause: LCM is caused by arenaviruses. Principle hosts or carriers of the virus are house mice. The virus is spread to humans by the feces, urine, or saliva of the hamster or food that has come in contact with it.

Treatment: LCM can only be determined by a blood test. The disease is rarely fatal for the hamster. Usually it will have recovered within three weeks.

With a plastic syringe like this you can administer medications or force-feed.

Questions about
Care and Health

? Does the hamster need an exercise wheel?

No, if the cage is big enough and has enough varied equipment, it does not necessarily have to have an exercise wheel. It is only important that the hamster have enough opportunity to make the most of its active drive. An exercise wheel can improve the hamster's temperament and well-being. According to new scientific studies, the hamster does not gain weight as easily with an exercise wheel, does not gnaw on the cage, and increases the number of babies for female hamsters.

? The food bowl is always empty. Is my hamster eating too much?

As a rule, a hamster eats only as much as it really needs. If it becomes too fat, it is mostly due to the type of the food being offered. When the food dish is always empty, do not forget that hamsters hoard. Search the cage thoroughly, especially in the corners or a favorite hiding place, and you may find that your pet has established a store. Otherwise, through regular weight monitoring, you will have a clear overview of its health.

? What are obsessive behaviors and how can I avoid them?

Obsessive behaviors are behavioral disturbances (see page 125). They appear as a consequence of improper maintenance conditions. Therefore, they are sometimes also described as compulsive movements. The animals can gnaw constantly on the cage wires, continually run in circles or back and forth over a particular stretch, or scratch incessantly in one corner of the cage. Either they are trying to calm themselves that way in the stress situations or the monotonous cage arrangement gives them no other opportunity to express their drive to move. The problem is that sometimes "ingrained" obsessive-compulsive behaviors can never be remedied, even by improved maintenance conditions. For this reason, arrange the cage equipment so that these behaviors do not develop. Otherwise an exercise wheel helps to reduce the compulsive movements.

? Can I give my pet a little piece of chocolate or a sour ball now and then?

No! You want your hamster to do well and to feel good, so it should not receive any supplementary food containing sugar. Metabolic disturbances leading to diabetes can be the result. Its life would be shortened by feeding it those well-meaning snacks. Instead, give your pet little pieces of apple, banana, or carrot; some unsweetened cottage cheese; or even a mealworm.

? May the hamster nibble on cartons or pieces of wood?

Yes, as a rule this is absolutely harmless to its health and actually provides variety. But caution is urged with printed or glued cartons and lacquered or treated wood. So use unprinted corrugated cardboard (best are the kind food was packed in), cardboard, and untreated wood.

? My hamster has been scratching himself a lot recently. What does this mean?

You should investigate the cause of every change in behavior. Frequent scratching can indicate mite infestation. Examine the skin and fur of the hamster very carefully to detect discolorations or changes in the skin. Mites and other skin parasites are often so small that one cannot see them with the naked eye, or only with difficulty. Take your pet to the veterinarian, who can make a definite diagnosis.

? My golden hamster has a black spot under the fur on its right and left sides. Is it sick?

No, the spots are only the so-called flank glands of the golden hamster. These secrete a waterproof fluid. Hamsters mark their burrow or their territory with it to signal that other hamsters should keep away. As the hamster moves along, it scrapes its side against an object or the wall of the cage in order to deposit the secretion. Dwarf hamsters have such glands on their abdomens. They slide over the ground briefly when marking.

? My hamster has diarrhea. What shall I do?

Stop giving it water-retaining fresh food and cottage cheese. Take it to the veterinarian as quickly as possible. He or she will give further advice about feeding. Ask for a medication that contains bacteria to rebuild the intestinal flora.

? Do hamsters have to drink?

Unfortunately, there is no clear answer to this question. If one provides sufficient fresh food, one can keep hamsters, especially dwarf hamsters, without additional water. But pregnant or nursing females, as well as sick hamsters should always have an easily reachable water bottle in the cage.

Activity
and Wellness

Boredom and too little exercise can cause illness. Therefore the hamster kept as a pet needs appropriate stimulus. For example, how about an adventure playground?

How to Keep Boredom at Bay

Just like humans, hamster do not like living in a confined, sparely furnished home.
You will be amazed at how much fun your hamster has in a variety-filled cage,
complete with opportunities for climbing and hiding.

Hamsters need a lot of exercise, although there are still no precise measurements from the wild as to how many yards or even miles per night a hamster can cover.

Always Active

To be sure, the most recent observations in the wild indicate that the hamster prefers the comforts of its burrow. But when you observe the hamster as a pet on its exercise wheel, it becomes clear that it is covering ground even in the cage (see page 98). Studies have shown that by attaching an infrared light (a device that is also used in alarm systems or to turn on a light by movement) to the cage, the golden hamster will actively run around its dark cage almost the whole time. This is obviously all the more possible when the cage is large and fully equipped. Of course, you can also increase your golden hamster's activity by allowing it to run free in the room (see page 103). The following pages include some possible activities that will keep your hamster busy in appropriate ways.

Do Hamsters Play?

Hamsters do not play as we humans do from time to time because they are really always on the lookout for places to hide, for food, or for a partner during breeding season. This investigative behavior is innate and essential for them to hold their own in the rather inhospitable natural environment in which they live.

As pets, they are supplied with food and shelter. In addition to its secure shelter with a sleeping house, it is very important and appropriate to offer your ham-

The view from the "tree house" is splendid for the cute little dwarf hamster. ▶

ster many opportunities to make the most of its inborn behavior program.

What Hamsters Like

The pet store offers a wide range of accessories for the hamster cage. Many of them are highly recommended. You can choose objects made from vegetable

Crawling in and out: Hamsters have an insatiable desire to creep in everywhere, or at least stick their heads inside holes or cracks. The pet store offers a multitude of items promoting such hamster activity, such as tubes of dried grass with openings for crawling in and out, wooden cubes with holes bored in several places, or tunnel-like hollow wooden rounds. Keep in mind that the openings for golden hamsters should be at least 2 in. (4.5 cm) across. Hamsters can

DID YOU KNOW THAT . . .

. . . golden hamsters in the wild are more active?

Laboratory hamsters or golden hamsters that are kept as pets run an average of 5,300 revolutions per day on the exercise wheel. Free-living hamsters surpass this performance more than three-fold. Recently imported wild golden hamsters achieved an impressive 16,800 revolutions. Therefore, wild golden hamsters are clearly more active.

raw materials like wood, sisal, or hemp. Another popular option is plastic. Carefully inspect the accessories to be sure that there are no projecting nails, screws, wiring, or similar sharp points that could injure your hamster (see page 105).

Climbing possibilities: Anyone who has observed hamsters in the wild as they ascend from their burrows with vertical escape tunnels knows that they like to climb. Various floor levels in the hamster home meet this need, as do little ladders, houses with several floors, or branches installed in the cage.

get stuck in smaller openings or narrow cracks.

Homemade

As an active hamster lover, you should try to offer your hamster homemade items. If you have never sawed or glued, there must certainly be someone in the family who can help. In any case, it has always been a lot of fun for me and provided a certain satisfaction when I could observe my hamster assuming ownership of the homemade things.

When buying or making accessories, consider what suits **the innate behavior** of the hamster and what is appropriate for it.

Tip: By researching on the Internet, you can find a whole list of building instructions for "toys" that other hamster lovers have already successfully completed. Here are only a few suggestions.

Wooden objects: Wood is, of course, the best material for this purpose. Wood scraps, which are inexpensive to obtain, are often satisfactory. You can use practically all types of wood (except cedar) and chipboard. You must just make sure that the wood and chipboard have not been chemically treated (wood preservatives, etc.). Ask your dealer. If possible, pieces of wood or chipboard should not be nailed or screwed because the animals gnaw on such metal pieces intensively and can loosen them. Cold wood glue with a water base is the best fastener. The most diverse accessories can be made of wood. Besides houses (see page 43), you can build such items as seesaws, ladders, platforms, and bridges. You must inspect connected moving parts very carefully because these are often sources of injury for the hamster.

Objects of clay/plasticine: Are you a potter? Then you can make little houses or caves out of modeling clay or non-toxic plasticine. Hamsters gladly take to houses or "fitness equipment" such as bridges or tubes. Make sure that the openings never measure less than 2 in. (4.5 cm) (preferably they should be larger, since the size can change during baking). Food dishes can be thrown or hand-built, too. Even more comfortable are handmade items of plasticine, which are air-dried and inexpensive. Check very carefully first to be sure that the material is nontoxic.

Papier-mâché technique: Build your hamster a cave using papier-mâché, or layers of dampened paper. Use an inflated balloon for the foundation, and glue several layers of newspaper over the balloon, one at a time. Use wallpaper paste for the glue. Allow the cave to dry after each layer. When it is dry and sturdy, paint the cave with water-soluble poster paint.

Cardboard cartons: Small cardboard cartons with "windows" and "doors" are very popular. Fastened together with glue, they become adventure play-

You can even stay at comfortable temperatures in an igloo.

grounds. When the cartons become soiled or chewed to pieces, simply replace them with new ones!

Total hamster fitness.
The exercise wheel provides movement, but it does not replace the big cage.

The Exercise Wheel— Better Than Its Reputation

The pros and cons of the exercise wheel in the hamster cage have been much debated already, and there is reason enough to scientifically examine its effects on the animals. I myself have

With the correct design the disputed running wheel provides for healthy exercise.
▼

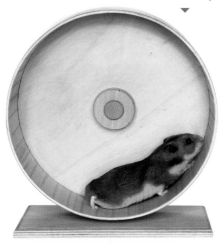

taken part in the studies on this subject. Our concept consisted first of offering the animals in small cages a chance to develop their natural drive for movement. Although to date no one knows exactly how much distance the hamster actually covers (this will eventually be studied in its habitat), a certain amount of movement can never hurt, either. After all, the animals voluntarily go onto the exercise wheel night after night and then also leave it again. In no case can it be said that an exercise wheel is "addictive," as is stated in some texts about hamsters. No hamster has collapsed in exhaustion on the exercise wheel because it can no longer leave of its own free will. On the contrary, one can tell by the number of revolutions whether the hamster might be sick or have some other problem.

On the basis of female hamsters' running performance, inferences can even be drawn about their readiness to mate. One does see a problem in that the exercise wheel is not "repercussion free," that is, when the hamster goes onto the exercise wheel, it is compelled, as it were, to keep on running by the inertia of the wheel (this is especially true for the larger hamsters). But since it does leave the wheel at various times and is by no means exhausted when it does so, this objection can perhaps be dismissed. In a scientific study, hamsters with and without exercise wheels were compared. It was determined that the hamsters with exercise wheels exhibited considerably fewer so-called obsessive-compulsive behaviors (resulting from boredom) such as gnawing on the cage or prolonged scratching.

Although we researchers had assumed that hamsters with an exercise wheel

THE MOST POPULAR "HAMSTER TOYS"

YOU CAN USE TO PLEASE YOUR HAMSTER

For crawling into	Tubes of dried grass; wooden cubes with several holes drilled through them; tunnel-like hollowed out wooden rounds or pottery tubes with various entrances and exits; cardboard tubes (from inside paper towel or toilet paper rolls)
For climbing	Large branches, which are simply fastened to the cage floor; wooden bridges and ladders; little houses of wood with different levels; tube systems with drainage pipes (see page 39)
For running	A large cage; exercise wheel (see page 98); a running course full of little hiding spots
For exploring	A shallow dish planted with edible grass or grain seed; a cave system of cartons linked by cardboard tubes (see page 97); a homemade labyrinth; homemade caves (see papier-mâché, page 97)

would lose weight through the fitness program, it turned out to be just the opposite: Animals with an exercise wheel were heavier than those without an exercise wheel. We were baffled at first. But then we examined the body composition of the hamsters more carefully. This is possible with a modern method that similarly determines human body fat by means of scales. And lo and behold, the hamsters with access to the exercise wheel had not become fatter but had developed more muscle mass. This we judged to be a clear indication that the exercise wheel improved the physical condition of the animals. So the installation of an exercise wheel in the cage, in my opinion,

can be recommended without reservation.

The proper exercise wheel: The larger and lighter the exercise wheel, the better. Experiments showed severe strains on the hamsters' spinal columns from exercise wheels with diameters that were too small. Therefore, for the golden hamster, the diameter of the running wheel should be at least 10 in. (25 cm), or ideally 12 in. (30 cm). For dwarf hamsters, 8 in. (20 cm) is the minimum. The width of the running wheel should be no less than 3⅓ in. (8 cm). Make sure that it has a solid running surface (see page 98).

Furthermore, the running wheel should be solid on one side. It should be

Perfect for Hamsters

▶ **1** **Exploring** is written large here. A construction like this one makes a hamster's heart beat faster. This is total activity for the small pet.

▶ **2** **The branching layout** invites crawling in and out. The holes can also be used as lookout ports.

▶ **3** **And after "work"** there is rest. It's possible to hide really well in the wooden tube and observe the surroundings.

attached from the outside to the cage wire on that side. The open side should have no exposed struts, which could cut the hamster's limbs like scissors. Some wheels begin to squeak after extensive use. Some petroleum jelly or cooking oil for the moving parts provides a good remedy here.

If you think your hamster is using the exercise wheel too often, you do not, of course, have to leave the wheel in the cage all the time.

Note: Not recommended are metal exercise wheels in which the animal has to run on wire bars. The hamster can too easily slip and suffer very serious injuries to its extremities.

Tube Systems

A few years ago, complete tube systems in fashionable colors with varied accessories became available in pet stores. Aside from the hefty price and the—for a true hamster lover—kitschy appearance, these systems are suitable for hamsters in a limited capacity. The tubes are sometimes too narrow for golden hamsters or too smooth or easily broken, which then could result in injury to the animals. But despite all that, you should not rule out piping systems fundamentally. They are very suitable as connections between cages or for mounting platforms. After all, hamsters in the wild live in such tubes in their burrows, so this coincides with their innate behavior. If you offer tubes to your hamster, you will quickly notice how the animal loves to rest in them. I have already mentioned tube systems in the chapter How Hamsters Like to Live (see page 30).

The best items to use are PVC pipes with a diameter of at least 2 in. (4.5 cm). Don't make the pipes too long; you'll need to allow for the required cleaning and air circulation. Shorter pieces are more appropriate for this purpose.

Playgrounds and Play Cages

If you have space available, connecting two cages is highly recommended. Then one cage can function as a sleeping cage and the dining area, and the other can be the adventure playground. Even better than a second cage is a self-contained room for the hamster. You can create different shapes with walls at least 12 in. (30 cm) high arranged around a floor board. A large hexagon connected with the sleeping cage is almost ideal. The room remains open at the top so that you can observe your hamster without difficulty. Put a layer of litter in the room and furnish it with toys.

Dangerous Toys

Carefully inspect all prospective toys for danger of injury, nontoxic materials, and sufficient air circulation in small containers. In this respect, the "hamster balls," "jogging balls," or "hamster cars" often offered in pet stores along with the brightly colored tube systems (see page 100) are anything but recommended. This type of activity for and with the hamster has nothing to do with proper hamster keeping! The animals are imprisoned in a tight container from which they cannot free themselves and cannot get air. They roll around the room uncontrollably and may possibly

TIP

Grass for hamsters

You can buy special grass in the pet store. This grass is sold as a set with seeds for you to sow or as a container of grass that is already growing. Hamsters love to hide in the grass, but they also find it tasty. Simply place the dish of grass in the hamster cage.

fall from a raised surface. Please spare your hamster this torture and instead observe your pet in as appropriate an environment as possible!
Of course, the hamster also has no place in a dollhouse or model train. Hamsters are living creatures and not toys!

A secure free run is a marvelous thing. After all, one can exercise properly here, and there are healthy treats besides. What more does a hamster want?
▼

Free Exercise Indoors

When your hamster gets lively in the evening, he will thoroughly enjoy a little excursion in the room. Here he can move extensively, explore the unknown, and follow new scents. And you can enjoy "hamster entertainment" live.

The most important rule is: Never let your hamster run free in the yard, in a meadow, on a balcony, or on a terrace!

No Exercise Outdoors!

Certainly you have already observed that guinea pigs or dwarf rabbits can be kept in special outdoor hutches in the garden. Unfortunately, we do not have this option with hamsters. It is too dangerous there for the small mammals. As is described in the chapter The Typical Hamster (see page 6), hamsters belong to the family of burrowing animals, so they could very easily burrow under the hutch. Also, they could find a little hole or a hiding place in the hutch caging and disappear, never to be seen again. Finally, diseases, such as parasites that establish themselves in a hamster's fur, can lurk outdoors.

Preparing for Free Exercise

If you want to provide your hamster with exercise, offer it a free run indoors. Even though there are a number of dangers lurking in the house, you can easily remove them.
Prepare the room: The floor should have a carpet. Parquet, laminated, or

similarly smooth surfaces are not suitable for the hamster to run on, unless you first cover the area with a sheet or tablecloth. A number of other restrictions are listed in the table "Sources of Danger During a Free Run in the Room" (see page 105). See to it that the dangers are removed, and nothing will stand in the way of the new hamster freedom. You can prevent the hamster from crawling under the furniture with strips of cardboard 12 in. (30 cm) high. A similar strip at the doors will allow you to leave the room briefly without the free walker escaping.

Don't use force!

You should proceed cautiously with the first free run. New surroundings mean stress for the hamster and make its heart rate increase (see page 53). Therefore, do not force your hamster to do anything.
Put the cage on the floor and open the cage door, "the door to the wide world" of the room. This is better than taking the hamster out of the cage; being grasped already means stress for your pet. Now, stay at a suitable distance, but do not let the hamster out of your sight. The hamster will gradually begin to explore the room. The advantage for you is that you will quickly learn to recognize the "weak spots" of your room

preparation and learn what areas still needs to be made secure or which objects should be removed.

Note: It is advisable to place a flexible wooden bridge from the cage down to the floor so that the hamster can exit the cage on its own. The hamster can run over it without catching a paw in the cage and injuring himself.

Be careful with free runs!
Your supervision is required in case the hamster encounters danger.

Variety During Free Exercise

When you have removed all the sources of danger and the first excursions into the room have gone well, create some

hamster-tailored diversion for the adventure seeker. The only limit here is your imagination. Below are a few tried-and-true suggestions, which will probably please your pet.

▶ Build a "hamster fort" in the middle of the room. This can be a shallow box with some litter and a way to enter (ladder or cutout door), where you put different accessories, such as seesaws, ladders, platforms, bridges, branches, stones, and little houses.
▶ Link different wooden parts together or lay tubes on top of one another with a rubber band around the middle.
▶ Using stones or pieces of wood, build a maze and put a healthy snack in the middle as a reward.
▶ Prepare a shallow dish with hamster grass or grain seeds and when the plants are 2–4 in. (5–10 cm) high, put it in the room as an edible snack.
▶ Lay a large branch on the floor with little pieces of carrot or cucumber fastened to the ends.
▶ Build a cave system by cutting holes in cartons and connecting the cartons with cardboard tubes (e.g., paper towel tubes).
▶ Offer your hamster a dish of sand or a mixture of wood shavings and peat in which it can dig and burrow. Hide little bits of food in the mixture so that the effort is rewarding for your pet.

Do not leave the hamster alone during these outings but closely supervise the free run. Perhaps you have overlooked a source of danger, or maybe the hamster will get into a desperate situation that requires your intervention. Expect, too, that the hamster will leave a few droppings now and again (formed pieces of

Now one has a heavy load to carry, and there are also obstacles on the way . . .
▼

SOURCES OF DANGER DURING A FREE RUN IN THE ROOM

Danger	Consequences	Avoiding the Danger
Poisonous houseplants (e.g., African violets, philodendron, dieffenbachia, ficus, azalea)	Signs of poisoning (e.g., drooling, labored breathing, convulsions), death	Place houseplants and cut flowers out of the hamster's reach
Exposed cords, outlets, power strips lying on the floor	Burns, fatal shocks	Put cords and power strips out of the hamster's reach; secure outlets with childproof covers
Slippery floors (laminate, parquet, linoleum, tile)	The hamster can slide on the smooth floor and be injured.	A carpet is ideal, or an old linen cloth (bed sheet) spread out for the free run
Open doors and reachable open windows	The hamster can get into another room or outdoors; being crushed when the door or window is suddenly closed.	Keep doors and windows closed during the free run
Other house pets such as cat and dog	Bite wounds	Shut out other house pets during the free run.
Sharp or pointed objects, also broken cage wires	Wounds, especially to the eyes	Leave no sharp or pointed objects lying around; inspect the cage often
Burning candles	Burns	Do without any burning candles
Open chinks, crevices, or gaps	Hiding, getting stuck, injuries	Close off access or add covering
Curtains or draperies hanging to the floor	Use as nest material; obstruction of the cheek pockets; toes hooking them	Provide material for upholstering the nest (see page 45) and keep an eye on the animal
Electrical equipment	Burns; fatal shock	Turn off electrical equipment; do not have any cords lying on the floor; pull all plugs
Poisonous substances (medications, household cleaners)	Poisoning	Make sure you put away toxic materials

MY HAMSTER

How does your hamster react to sounds?

The Russian scientist Pavlov discovered that animals can associate different stimuli. Try testing this with your golden hamster.

The test begins:

Every time you give the hamster a special snack, make a noise. Make sure you always give the snack in the same place. After about ten such feedings, give just the signal without offering food. Did the hamster learn to respond to the signal only? You may see that it interrupts all activities and looks around for the expected snack.

My test results:

excrement), but these do not harm your floor covering. They are dry and can be easily sucked up by the vacuum cleaner. Sometimes you might notice a few drops of urine, but this is the exception to the rule. Research has shown that the hamster normally attends to its bathroom needs during the resting period.

A Sand Bath Is Fun

Offer your hamster a shallow dish of sand to roll in. Its coat is cleaned by the sand bath and possible parasites (mites) are removed by it. Chinchilla sand is best for this purpose. Thanks to a special process, the grains of sand are round. Never use builder's or play sand, since it can damage the hairs of the fur.

You may discover that your hamster ignores the sand bath completely. This is not very unusual. You will simply find out this way that your hamster rejects sand baths. After all, your pet should not be forced into anything.

Some Tips for Observation During Free Exercise

Put out food: Hamsters hoard. And you can observe them doing this on the free run. Scatter little bits of food and watch how they are stuffed into the cheek pouches and collected. Preferably place the food in a somewhat raised location so that the animal has to stretch up to get to it.

How fast the hamster runs: How long does it take the hamster to collect its food? Figure out how fast your hamster travels! Measure a distance of 2 or 3 yards (2 or 3 m), and clock the time the hamster needs to cover it. You need only divide the measured seconds by the length of the stretch and you have the speed of the runner in yards (meters) per second. More comparable to the speed of humans are miles (kilometers) per hour. A person goes about 3.1 mi/h (5 km/h). The calculation is easy: Take the meters per second of the hamster times 3.6 and you already have the speed of the hamster in kilometers per hour. Who is faster: human or hamster?

Little training practice: You can also try to condition the hamster to colors. Use two different-colored containers for food. The colors should be sharply differentiated, since the hamster can only process brightness values. Place the dishes side by side, but always put the food in the same dish. After a time change the locations of the dishes. Did the hamster note which color meant food? Or did it only respond to the placement of the dishes? Of course, the food should be as scentless as possible so that it does not detect it from far away.

The sand bath is especially beloved by the dwarf hamsters and should never be missing from their cage.

▼

When Hamsters Have Babies

7

The birth and raising of hamster babies is certainly a fascinating experience. But before you decide to take on such a large responsibility, you should know where the babies are going in the future.

Hamster Mating and the Birth of Young

Granted, it is delightful to experience the results of a hamster mating, to see the tiny babies in the nest and witness their rapid development. But what happens to the young when they are independent? Will you have room for even one of them?

Anyone who wants to breed hamsters needs some technical knowledge as well as the required space. But the primary and potentially large problem is the question of where all the young are going to go after being weaned from their mother. And so it would be best not to give advice on breeding here. There are licensed, professional hamster breeders who are annually inspected by the official veterinarians and have a contract-regulated market for the young. Besides, in view of the various breeds that have come to exist, it is especially important not to breed at random. For one thing, the breeds cannot be maintained this way, and for another, the health and life span of the hamster can be adversely affected.

Unexpected Offspring

Naturally, it can happen that you choose an especially pretty and sturdy female from a breeder or in the pet store. You are happy that the hamster lady eats so well and keeps gaining weight. Then one day you go to the hamster cage, find out that Mrs. Hamster is not anywhere to be seen today, and suddenly hear some strange squeaking from the little hamster house. A look into the house brings an enormous surprise! Babies have arrived! There are eight little pink hamster babies lying helpless—being nursed by the mother—in their cozy nest. What do you do? It will be good for you to read further at this point and be well prepared to calmly face the raising and development of the young (see page 115). It really isn't that difficult to rear the unplanned hamster litter.

Hamsters are so-called nidicolous animals, which are completely helpless when they come into the world. In the first weeks of life, they are dependent on their mother. ▶

When breeding golden hamsters, you must make sure that the female is in the **mating mood**. Otherwise males and females must be separated immediately.

Hamster Mating in the Wild and in the Cage

In the wild, after they have spent the entire winter in the burrow, the golden hamsters come to the surface in March to look around for fresh food and a potential mate. Besides the increasing temperatures, the longer hours of daylight lure them out of the burrow. The males are probably the more active sex; they run down several females' burrows to see if the lady hamsters are in the mood for reproduction. This happens every 4 days with hamsters. Then one day, they are ready to mate with a male from about an hour before sunset until noon the next day. This characteristic change of behavior of the female is termed estrus. It was Hera, the wife of the Greek god Zeus, who sent an insect, a horsefly—*oestrus* in Greek—to harass her husband's beloved after Zeus had changed his adored Io into a snow-white cow. The cow restlessly sought to escape her tormentor. The term for the restlessness of the female during the reproductive phase has its source in this myth.

The mating ritual

Female hamsters are also more than twice as active in the night of estrus than in the other nights of their cycle. If a male appears, there is a brief, reciprocal sniffing of noses and of the genital regions of both partners. Then the female remains standing, bends her back, and raises her bottom. This characteristic mating position is termed *lordosis,* when the female invites the male to mate. But, on the other hand, if the female is not ready to mate, fighting can occur. A breeder will place the male in the cage of the female each evening and must immediately separate both animals if the female is not in estrus. The mating can last all night; sometimes females even mate with several males during a single night. According to recent studies, the female chooses her partner if possible. This choice is less about strength and beauty. It is important that the male have genes as different as possible from those of the female, so that the genes of the offspring are completely new mix-

At three weeks and after the eyes have opened, it's time to investigate the environment.

▼

tures and are thus less susceptible to pathogenic organisms or parasites. The male mounts up to 50 times and impregnates the female. After a successful mating, the female will no longer tolerate the male in her burrow and drives him out. In the cage, if he is not removed immediately after the mating, he can be so badly attacked by the female that he dies of his wounds. This essentially goes for mating of Chinese

▶ Campbell's dwarf hamster
▶ Roborovski dwarf hamster
▶ Djungarian dwarf hamster

Unfortunately there are no observations of the behavior in the wild. Going back to the findings of Canadian researchers, we have assumed until now that the males of Campbell's dwarf hamster, in particular, remain in the vicinity of the

DID YOU KNOW THAT . . .

. . . females are only ready to mate for a very short period of time?

Female hamsters are ready to mate every four days from approximately March to September for about ten hours. We term such animals polyestrous. Sometime around midnight of estrus (see page 110) the egg cells are automatically set free in the female. The ability to reproduce is controlled by, among other things, the rhythm of the days. If it is light for fewer than 11 hours per day, reproduction shuts down.

striped hamsters as well, as the male is seldom tolerated after mating and should be removed.

Phodopus Dwarf Hamsters Are Different

The expulsion of the male after mating has not been observed in the three *Phodopus* species described in this book, when they are kept as pets. With these three species, you should try—provided there is a large-enough cage—to leave the male with the female. The species are

birth nest and help with the raising of the young. But these findings obviously were the result of the small cage that was used. There the males had no choice and had to remain in the vicinity of the nest. If the pair is kept in a sufficiently large cage, however, another picture appears. The role of the father in the three *Phodopus* species was examined in the most recent studies by scientists at the University of Halle. The pairs were kept in sufficiently large cages, and the males even had the opportunity to seek out another sleeping house placed in the cage.

◀ *To young dwarf hamsters, sunflowers are as big as giant sequoias are to humans.*

The exit from the nest box was constantly monitored by a small camera. The result was somewhat surprising. The greatest interest in the young was shown by the father of the Roborovski dwarf hamsters. With the other species, it was exactly the opposite of what had been expected. Most of the time, the Djungarian males were in the nest box of the young, while the Campbell fathers showed the least interest in their offspring. They preferred sleeping outside the nest box in their own sleeping houses.

Pregnancy and Birth

After mating, the female begins to prepare a nest for the young by upholstering it with soft material.

Padding material for the nest

The hamster breeder will place additional material at the female's disposal. The animals especially enjoy soft cellulose (paper tissues). They will ignore the best food when they can fill their cheek pouches with such practical, soft padding materials.

Length of pregnancy

The gestation period of the female hamster is one of the shortest of all mammals. Golden hamster mothers bring their young into the world after 16 days. Dwarf hamsters need 2 days longer, and the pregnancy of the Chinese striped hamster lasts 20 to 22 days.

Diet during pregnancy

The female must take in much protein-rich food during pregnancy. Therefore,

give her cottage cheese, fresh cheese, or insect food daily. Fresh food should always be offered as well. Many breeding attempts run into problems because the expectant mothers are not properly nourished. The females also eat more than usual, and toward the end of pregnancy they become increasingly quiet or hardly leave their burrow or sleep house. They must not be disturbed during this period or taken out of the cage at all. Obviously major cage cleaning must be postponed.

The birth

Then one morning it is over. As with most mammals, with the exception of humans, birth frequently takes place during a time of rest. When birthing, the mother needs absolute quiet. Even the tiniest disturbance can affect the birth. First-time mothers, especially, will break off the birthing or not take care of the young. Also, eating of the young is a frequent occurrence. Of course, the mother should not be held responsible for this, since it is a protective mechanism determined by nature to avoid the unnecessary energy for a litter that cannot survive. The birth takes about an hour. Rodents, to which the hamsters belong, have a womb or a uterus (as the biologists call it) that has two parts. The little hamster young are lined up inside like pearls on a necklace, so each part of the uterus contains several young. At birth, which is very stressful for the hamster mother, the babies are expelled one after the other. On average, a golden hamster mother gains eight, pink, blind, helpless animals. With females that are bearing young for the first time, in particular, the number of babies is often smaller. By the second or third litter, more young animals are born. The record to date is seventeen young. The average number is only slightly fewer with dwarf hamsters. The young are born blind and naked, technically termed *nidicolous*. In the beginning they are completely helpless. In the wild, of course, the birth takes place in the mother's burrow. The mother eats the fetal envelope and the umbilical cord. Do not be frightened if the shavings or nesting material becomes somewhat bloody in the vicinity of the birth. This is completely normal. Immediately after the birth, the mother begins to lick the young in order to stimulate their metabolism. It does not take long, and the young receive their first mother's milk. The mother hardly leaves the nest in the first few days, since the young are nursing and must be kept warm above all. In the first stages of their lives, the little ones are still not able to regulate their own body temperature. As with all mammals, this must be about 98.6°F (37°C) so that all the body functions can proceed.

Golden Hamster Mating

▶ 1 **The female** bends her back forward and presents her genital opening. She takes the characteristic mating position (lordosis). The male is still inexperienced and tries to mount her from the side.

▶ 2 **The mating is thus completed.** The several mountings of the male ensure the success of the mating. The females are quite patient when they are in the mating mood.

Raising the Young Animals

Normally the hamster mother is a model provider for her little ones.
Within four weeks the young hamsters are finally so independent
that they can live without their mother.

Undoubtedly you are impatient and would love to look at the babies in the nest. Now is when a sleeping nest with a removable roof proves its worth.

A Careful Look into the Nest

About six hours after the birth, you can cautiously take a quick look into the nest and satisfy your curiosity at last. It's a clever idea to lure the mother out of the house beforehand with something delicious, such as a dandelion leaf. Rapidly count the babies and close the house again. The mother will come back quickly, since she is usually being called by her young. You didn't hear anything? No wonder, for the babies make sounds of abandonment in the ultrasonic range, which are not audible to either humans or predators.
You should inspect the young daily, with caution advised. The mother begins nursing the young right after birth. During this period, she has an increased need for fluid. So give her many fresh feedings, or make sure that the water bottle is always filled with fresh water.

The Little Ones Become Big

The development of the young proceeds quickly. Even by the second day of life, the backs of young, wild-colored golden hamsters grow increasingly gray, and on the fourth day their entire backs are covered with a fluff of hair. By the fifth day, the first light brown hairs appear, and by the seventh day their little bodies are entirely covered.
By the sixteenth day, the little hamsters are fully colored, though their fur is still somewhat thinner than their mother's at first. The slow growth of the fur on the naked-born young animals allows the animal's flank glands to be seen, which can be difficult to do in grown animals because of the thick fur. By the

TIP

Who would like a hamster?

It is not easy to find the right homes for a litter of young hamsters. As a human "foster parent," you really should make sure you know what your hamster offspring may expect in their new home. This is not possible when you give them to a pet store, though it may be your only option.

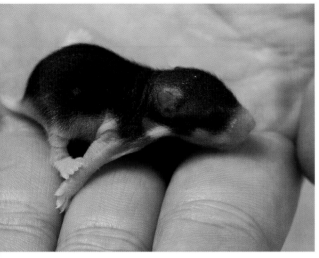

▲

This golden hamster baby is one week old.
Fur growth has already begun. The eyes are
still closed.

second day, the flank glands are already shining through the skin as light spots. These have become noticeably larger by day seven and now look more brownish yellow, before they grow darker.

The first sense the young hamsters develop is the sense of smell. Even at the age of five days, the young recognize the smell of their nest when they have a choice among different scents. The auditory canal opens from the fourth day and the outer ear unfolds. However, it takes a long time, up to about the seventeenth day of life, before the hamster can move its ear muscles. On the thirteenth day, the first young hamsters begin to open their eyelids, and after two and a half weeks they should all have their eyes open. On the second day, the forelegs of the young hamster begin to shove the body forward to get to the mother's nipples. But the little

animals are not yet able to turn themselves over from the back position; this first becomes possible on the seventh day. Then they can also hold their heads up longer and try to get some impression of their surroundings. From the tenth day on, the little hamsters are already able to creep forward. Usually one side functions better than the other, so that the little ones always crawl in circles. When they come to a drop-off, they can perceive it with their vibrissae, the sensory hairs, and draw back. Starting on the thirteenth day, the young can sit up and take in solid food by holding small morsels of food with their front paws. Grooming with their front paws is now possible, too. Incidentally, it is not odd but normal that the young hamsters sometimes eat their own balls of feces or their mother's. They satisfy their increased mineral requirements this way. After two weeks, the little hamsters can explore the cage on wobbly legs, and a few days later, their movement equals that of the adult animals.

Calendar of Development of Young Golden Hamsters

▶ First day (birth): Skin reddish to pink, eyes closed with lids stuck together, weight about 0.09 oz (2.5 g).

▶ Second day: Hints of gray hair, flank glands visible, front legs move.

▶ Third to fourth day: Gray hairs increase, outer layers of ear unfolds, the auditory canal opens, whiskers (vibrissae) clearly visible, weight about 0.12 oz (3.5 g).

▶ Fifth day: Light brown hairs visible, outer layer of ear against the head,

The Development of the Young
at a Glance

The First Few Days

Newborn hamster babies come into the world naked and blind. They must be warmed and suckled by the mother. In three or four days, the fur is already beginning to grow.

The First Excursions

At the age of one week, the first daring excursions away from the nest begin. But the mother immediately seizes the escapees in her mouth by the fold at the nape of the neck and carries them back to the secure nest.

Independent

After two weeks, the little ones' eyes slowly open. Now there is nothing standing in the way of the careful exploration of their surroundings. At three weeks the young are almost independent.

MY HAMSTER

Are there behavioral differences in a hamster litter?

Hamsters develop little personalities and characters of their own. They are more or less active, anxious, or daring. Some learn fast, while others take to things slowly. You can test this in your hamster's young.

The test begins:

You must mark the young individually. Use food coloring to paint a foot of the little ones. At about the eighteenth day of the babies' life, put new objects into the cage and note the order in which they are discovered by the young animals. Repeat this test over several days. Are the same ones always the first? Are there some who show only very little interest?

My test results:

back legs support the body, own nest is recognized by scent.

▶ Sixth day: Propels self with front and back legs, weight about 0.18 oz (5 g).

▶ Seventh day: Head is lifted, independent turning around from back position possible, beginning of solid food intake.

▶ Eighth day: Palpebral fissure (i.e., space between eyelids) visible, fur development on belly begins, weight about 0.25 oz (7 g).

▶ Ninth to tenth day: Black striping on back, circular locomotion, drop-off avoidance behavior (see page 14).

▶ Eleventh day: Back legs are drawn under the body, attempts to stand up.

▶ Twelfth day: Light brown coloration, weight about 0.42 oz (12 g).

▶ Thirteenth to fourteenth day: Color is approaching that of the mature animals, wobbly-legged movements, eyes beginning to open.

▶ Fifteenth to sixteenth day: Eyes open, coloring like mature animals.

▶ Seventeenth day: Ears erect, weight about 0.78 oz (22 g).

▶ Eighteenth day: Movement like mature animals.

▶ Twentieth day: Fur-like mature animals.

▶ Twenty-first day: Only solid food, weight about 1.16 oz (33 g), independent.

- Four weeks: Are separated from the mother.
- Five to six weeks: Placed in individual cages.

Who Leaves Whom?

The nursing of the young animals lasts for about three weeks in all hamster species. After that the mother's milk production stops and the young ingest solid food exclusively. Their diet now is no longer any different from that of the mature animals. The young remain with their mother for about a week longer. Just recently an interesting discovery has been made in the wild, which came about with the development of a means for marking individual pets. In this process, dogs, cats, and also smaller animals like hamsters have a tiny chip inserted under the skin. This process is largely painless for the animal. The chip is about the size of a grain of rice. Each chip is different, and it is possible to identify individual animals with a special reading device. After a hamster has been caught, it is marked and then set free. A plastic ring containing the antenna is placed at the opening of the burrow, and this is in turn connected to a signaling system. Each time the hamster enters or leaves the burrow, it is registered, and the results are noted. So one can find out which hamsters stay in which burrows—a wonderful thing! But what does this have to do with young hamsters? Until now, people have thought that the mother drives the young out of the burrow when they are old enough. With the new technique, we believe we have found out that it is just the other way around. The mother leaves the burrow in order to place it at the disposal of her young. The reason could be that the finished burrow still offers the young protection against predators before they are grown and can dig their own burrows. So for breeders of hamsters, they should really take the mother out of the cage and leave it for the young.

In practice, however, the four-weeks-old young are separated from the mother but are left together for another two weeks. Then, when the fighting grows increasingly worse, it is time for each hamster to go its own way.

Well, how fantastic! Standing up already works perfectly and the grooming procedure is already familiar, too.
▼

Questions About Birth and Development

? **Why do mother hamsters sometimes eat their children?**

This can occur especially when the mother hamster is still very young and inexperienced when she has her first litter. It is a natural defense mechanism that has come about in the course of the development of the species. Usually the mother hamster feels threatened or so stressed that she no longer sees any chance of survival for her young. In those circumstances, she will then waste no more energy on brood care, nursing, and the like. Rather, a new litter will be cared for later under better conditions. With a new litter, the mother can better evaluate the environment and will not be so sensitive. Therefore it does not depend on you entirely. However, you should check to see if the source of any sort of disturbance in the area around the birthing cage needs to be removed. Mother hamsters are especially sensitive to sounds (television, radio, frequent walking past the cage, etc.). Another reason can be protein deficiency during pregnancy and rearing. Be particularly careful to provide a balanced diet for the mother during this period. In very rare cases, eating the young is also attributable to a behavioral disturbance.

? **Must I remove the exercise wheel from the cage when the hamster mother is pregnant or has young?**

No, that is not necessary. Toward the end of her pregnancy, of her own accord, the mother-to-be runs on the exercise wheel less often and does not use it while she is nursing the young. On the other hand, when the young are big enough, they will try to go on the exercise wheel on their own and participate in the *fitness program* from the very beginning.

? **What should I consider if I want to breed baby hamsters?**

First off, you should be clear about where the young animals are going to go. Hamsters are relatively easy to breed, so that it can be difficult to find a taker for the offspring. They have a short pregnancy and development period. By six weeks after the mating of their mother, the young hamsters must be removed and kept separated by gender. Soon the animals in these same-sex groups will no longer get along, and they must be separated. If the placement of the young hamsters is settled, learn exactly what happens in the process of mating. Especially with golden hamsters, you must not keep males and females together for more than this brief period (approximately six hours). Also, different breeds should not mate, nor should hamsters from the same breed that show incompatibility. Moreover,

you must of course be knowledgeable about the requirements of the mother and her offspring during birth and development.

? Won't the mother miss her young when I remove them after four weeks?

No, the separation of the young animals is an utterly natural process. It does not compare with the mother-child bond of humans. As soon as the young are independent, the mother hamster has fulfilled her biological function and can perhaps take care of a new litter. Furthermore, recent studies have shown that in the wild it is not the children but the mother who first leaves the hamster burrow forever. Perhaps she makes the sheltering burrow available until the young become strong enough to dig their own holes to live in.

? How long should I leave the young with their mother?

For all the hamster species in this guide, the nursing period of the mother lasts for about three weeks. After that, milk production stops. One can then still leave the young with their mother for about one week, but they should be separated (removed) from her at the age of four weeks at the latest. If male and female siblings are kept together for more than five weeks, the females could become pregnant. Under observation, it is possible to keep same-sex groups together a little bit longer. If they become increasingly quarrelsome, they must be removed to individual cages.

? The hamster babies are eating the mother's droppings. Should I prevent this?

No, this is quite natural. The digestive organs of the young hamster after birth are not quite so perfectly arranged that they can digest all the necessary nutrients on their own. The mother's feces, on the other hand, contain easily accessible minerals, vitamins, and bacteria. For the young hamsters, these represent a good food supplement to build up their own intestinal flora.

? In my male hamster, the testicles are clearly visible and perhaps swollen. Is this dangerous?

Not at all! Especially in summer, in warmer temperatures, the testicles move to the outside for cooling. They must not become too warm or sperm development is impaired. Moreover, the size of the testicles alters with the yearly rhythm. In winter, hamsters in the wild do not reproduce, and they then have smaller testicles, which become larger again in spring and summer.

What to Do When There Are Problems

Most of the problems that arise when hamsters and humans live together are not the animal's fault, but instead are the result of errors in maintenance.

The Right Way to Solve Maintenance Problems

Golden hamsters and dwarf hamsters are robust and are really "easy-care" pets. Sometimes, however, problems with keeping hamsters do arise. This chapter contains advice on how to handle such situations properly.

The "Escape Artist"

As you were inspecting the cage thoroughly, has the hamster ever escaped? Or has it had a free run in the room and you then could not find it? The first rule is to keep calm and not chase the animal through the house. A hot pursuit will immediately wipe out the trust that has built up between you and the animal.

You see it: If you know where the hamster is hiding, you can try to get it to crawl into a container. For example, a shoebox or a similar rectangular box (e.g., a milk carton) in which you have cut out one of the ends is very good for this purpose. A pail or another container with a round opening is not suitable because the hamster will undoubtedly find a gap between floor and the round opening. Hold the container parallel to the floor at some distance behind the hamster and push your hand at it from the front. If you are lucky, the little hamster will turn around and run straight into the sheltering container.

You know that the hamster is in the room: If you have no idea exactly where the hamster is holed up in the room, it must be lured with food—preferably with its favorite food. With a longer absence, fresh foods (pieces of apple or melon) are—in my experience—the most successful bait. If you are not able to place the hamster cage on the floor so that the hamster can run into it, you need a "trap." If you intend to wait until the hamster runs into the trap on its own, the shoebox trap described at the left will do as will a long tube (e.g., a mailing tube for posters). Using a carrying cage (see page 53) is even better. Put some litter from the hamster's cage in the carrying cage and place the hamster's sleep house in it. Then put the food in the carrying cage and wait

Someone has ▶ *forgotten to close the cage here. Nothing like getting away!*

patiently until the little escapee can no longer resist. But if you cannot or will not wait, or want to try to catch it at night during its active period, you need a self-triggering trap. This can be a live trap, which is available from the pet store. These have a drop door attached to a movable floor plate. The food is put at the back of the trap so that the hamster has to run in to get it. When it runs over the center of the floor plate, the plate tips slightly to the rear and frees the drop door, which closes the entrance. This is a very gentle method of capture.

But you can also construct a trap yourself. Put some litter from the cage in the bottom of a bucket and on top of it a piece of apple or melon. Now lay a board against the bucket in such a way that the hamster can run right up it. A second board leads from the ramp down into the bucket. When the hamster scents the food, it climbs into the bucket, you remove the boards, and the hamster can comfortably be transferred to its permanent cage. If this doesn't work, place a cloth over the opening of the bucket and place food on it. The animal climbs up the ramp made by board laid from the floor outside to the rim of the bucket in order to get the food. Now it falls into the bucket along with the cloth.

You do not know where the hamster is: In all the rooms where your hamster might possibly be, place pieces of food overnight (raisins, sunflower seeds, peanuts) and close the doors. The next morning you can check to see where some of the food has been eaten. If you have no other free-living small rodents as housemates, you know where the escapee is and can place the trap there. **Note:** It is probably obvious that you should not punish the hamster for its breakout. It will never make the connection between its transgression and the punishment. On the contrary, it has only behaved the way his genetic program prescribed. Instead, be glad that you have such a clever and lively household companion.

The Hamster Bites and Will Not Become Trusting

Will your hamster not allow you to touch it? Does it flee or try to bite? When it has free run, does it immediately creep into the farthest corner and not come out again?

This behavior indicates that your hamster is either very young or has had a

◀ *A runaway may possibly be lured with food. Delicious fresh food is extremely attractive to the little pet.*

bad experience with humans at some time. If you haven't had your hamster for long, it is possible that the atmosphere in the sales cage or salesroom is the cause of such behavior. By nature, young hamsters are very lively, squeak, and will try to bite in danger. If, on the other hand, the hamster is older or has been with you a while, the problem can be due to something else that has caused much stress. Has it always gotten enough sleep? Or is it being disturbed during the day? Possibly someone has tried to pick it up while it was sleeping or maybe took it out of the cage? Or is the cage in a busy spot, perhaps beside a

Note: A problem can arise when the hamster has bitten a stranger, like one of your friends or an acquaintance. As the animal's keeper you are legally responsible for it. If, however, the hamster has been purposely agitated or provoked beforehand, the blame lies in large part with the one who was bitten.

Stereotypical Behaviors

Stereotypes are compulsive, repetitive ways of behaving that can sometimes appear in animals in human captivity. Predatory cats' running back and forth, always in the same path along the cage

To avoid mistakes in maintenance, you must know a lot
about the requirements of hamsters and
come to terms with their nature.

radio or television that is always on? Are there other loud noises in the vicinity of the hamster?
When you have checked all these things and eliminated them, the only help left is patience, patience, patience.... You must try to approach the hamster again and again, as described in Welcome Home (see page 56).
Speak quietly to the animal, for there are indications that it recognizes your voice. Try not to touch the hamster in the beginning but do offer little treats. It may take a long time (the older the hamster, the longer the time) before it becomes calm again. Also, hamsters are individuals. Some have a gentle and trusting nature, others remain cautious and anxious all their lives.

bars, or the oscillating behavior of the polar bears or elephants in zoos are examples of this.
When hamsters gnaw on the cage wire constantly, scratch incessantly in a corner, run back and forth along the side of the cage, or repeatedly leap up in a corner of the cage, it is an indication of the presence of such behavioral stereotypes. The cause is almost always, besides a cage that is too small, an inadequate supply of equipment to prevent boredom in the cage.
▸ Grant your hamster a large cage with several levels (see page 33) and a variety-filled arrangement of equipment (see page 40).

Pet Day at School

"My daughter's teacher would like to have 'pet day.' This way, the pupils are supposed to become acquainted with different pets. Our daughter would like to take her hamster. Is this really a good idea?"

Here I can only answer with a clear no. Basically there is nothing wrong with the idea of children in school becoming acquainted with the nature of pets. On the contrary, show-and-tell lessons are often responsible for pupils remembering more information than with theoretical lessons. But what may be possible with guinea pigs or dwarf rabbits stresses the hamster beyond all measure.

Stress can be fatal

The contact with several children is so stressful for the hamster that in the worst case its already limited life span can suffer from it. Some hamsters have died shortly after such an odyssey. Furthermore, the same thing applies to bringing the hamster to visit friends. Explain to your child that the hamster is an animal for observation and does not like to be shown around or handled by several people. Instead, allow your child to invite friends over to observe together, and encourage him or her to let them share in the delight of the small pet.

Do hamsters become friends?

If your child's friends also have hamsters, then the idea will certainly come up to have the hamsters play together. Talk your child out of this carefully but firmly. You know that hamsters are definitely loners. A strange hamster, no matter what sex it is, is always an intruder who must be fought. Such a confrontation means a terrible strain on both animals and should be avoided. Instead, urge your child and her friend or friends to compare results of observing their hamsters. Are they similar in behavior? What characteristics and preferences are shown? Maybe let your child exchange an object or some litter from both hamster cages and observe how the respective hamsters react to the scent. Get your child to compare and measure the amount of time the hamster spends on a new object and on an element from the alien hamster cage. Is there a difference when the objects carry the scent of a strange hamster?

▸ Let your hamster run free in the room from time to time, too, so that it can explore new environments.
▸ Do not always feed it in the same place but hide bits of food in different places in the cage or during free runs.

In zoos, they are now gradually converting to the practice of giving up firm feeding times and considering how the animals can "earn" their food.

Perhaps you have already heard the term *enrichment*, which is making the rounds in the zoo-keeping world. Behind this catchword hides an animal-keeping concept. It concerns the enrichment of the animals' daily life with imaginative ideas to combat the boredom of captivity. Also part of enrichment—that is the enrichment of the daily zoo routine—is offering the animals variety in their structured enclosures.

Once the hamster has become accustomed to such "kinks," that is, stereotypical behaviors, it will take quite a while until it exhibits normal behavior patterns again.

Note: More and more scientific studies are being carried out on the theme of enrichment in animal keeping. They compare animals that live under stimulus-poor conditions with those that are housed in cages with many accessories. From these studies, it has become clear that mice in meagerly equipped cages have decreased brain development. They show more stereotypical behavior and are more anxious. These are results that can be definitely transferred to hamster keeping.

Surprise—Suddenly There Are Baby Hamsters in the Cage

Shortly after you bought your hamster in the pet store, you find it one morning with newborn hamsters in the cage. The animals in the sales cage are displayed in groups. So it is definitely possible that the female, which you obvi-

Gnawing on the ▸ *cage bars is a compulsive behavior. It indicates too little variety in the cage setup or too small a cage.*

ously then have, was impregnated at the dealer's.

My recommendation is to try, if possible, to raise the young to an age of four weeks. That is nowhere near as difficult as you perhaps think in the first few moments. In the chapter When Hamsters Have Babies (see page 115), you will find detailed instructions for taking care of the new family. Immediately returning the hamster mother to the store, together with her babies, is not advisable. It means considerable stress for her, which can even end with her killing her young. Besides, it is very interesting to observe the upbringing of the young. The best thing to do is to notify the pet dealer right after the birth of the babies. Surely the dealer will agree to take the young hamsters when they are weaned so that their adoption is assured. Perhaps the dealer will even offer to contribute a small amount toward your additional expense.

The Sick Hamster Must Be Cared For

I have already described the possible diseases of hamsters in the chapter Well-cared for and Totally Healthy. But what can you do for the little one to promote its recovery? What special measures should be taken if it is really sick?

No temperature changes! If the hamster has caught cold or has diarrhea, you should be especially careful to keep a constant temperature of over 68°F (20°C) in its cage. Avoid drafts! Use a heat lamp. But make sure that the temperature at any spot in the cage never rises beyond 86°F (30°C).

For this reason, place the heat lamp at some distance from the cage wires. But take care that there are also areas with lower temperatures in the cage besides the warm ones. These offer the patient a place to which it can withdraw and protect itself from overheating.

After the hamster has spent some time in the heat, use an eye dropper to place a drop of water on each eye and in the nose area. This way you can prevent the dehydration of these sensitive areas.

Touch only when necessary! Avoid touching the hamster, for this causes additional stress (see page 56). However, there is an exception to this rule. You may have to administer medications to the animal, or may need to force-feed it due to poor appetite.

Administering medications: In giving medicines and in force-feeding, you must administer it directly into the hamster's mouth. A reliable aid for this is a disposable syringe (1 ml), which you fill with the medication dissolved in water or chamomile tea or with a "booster gruel." You must only try to

---

TIP

Bitten on the finger!

It can happen that the hamster unexpectedly bites into your finger when you pick it up. In shock, you may try to fling the animal away from you. Do not do that, as the hamster can be severely injured by that. Immediately place it on a firm surface, and it will let go, guaranteed.

These young golden hamsters have been raised together, but they must soon be separated.

force-feed during the hamster's waking phase. It is best if you do it with a helper. Hold the hamster with one hand placed on top and behind the front legs. The hand should wrap around the hamster's underbody without squeezing it. The second person should open its mouth and introduce the syringe behind the incisors and empty it. Only administer small portions at a time and give the hamster time to swallow. No more than 1 ml of gruel should be given per mealtime. If you are uncertain, it is better for the animal if you consult a veterinarian, who can show you the technique or, preferably, advise you otherwise.

Recipe for a booster gruel: Produce a gruel by pulverizing some of your hamster's usual grain feed (do not change its diet) in a mortar, enriching it with some banana or milk-free baby food,

and diluting it in lukewarm water. If the hamster rejects gruel, you can sweeten it with some honey. There are also special gruels in powder form, which you can get from your veterinarian.

Eating independently: After or even during the forced-feeding, the hamster must be urged to take in solid food on its own again. Your hamster may become used to the administration of the gruel diet and refuse to eat on its own. Tempt it with its favorite food (a dandelion leaf, for instance) by letting it sniff it over and over. At some point, if you are very patient, the hamster will be induced to snap at the food held in front of it.

Hamsters are not cuddly animals, so you should not pick up your pet all the time and carry it around. But when you do carry it, this is the way to do it.

All About Vacations and Aging

When buying a hamster, you never think: What am I going to do with my hamster when I go on vacation or if I get sick? And what will I do when my hamster is old and I have to say good-bye to it?

Planning for a weekend excursion? That is no problem for the hamster keeper, for the little animal can get along without you for two to three days. A prerequisite for this is that the animal should be provided with sufficient grain feed or lab blocks and that its water bottle is freshly filled. Check carefully once more before you leave to be sure that the cage is tightly closed all around and that no water is leaking out of the bottle. Set the heating or air conditioning so that the temperature in the room never rises or falls extremely. During the summer, you should draw the curtains or pull down the shades in the hamster's room.

Hamster on Vacation?

If you are planning a long absence, there are basically four possibilities that are fair to the hamster.

The hamster travels with you: If you are traveling within the country in the car and your new place of destination allows it, you can take the hamster along in its regular cage. The transport cage (see page 53) is too small for a long trip! In the summer, make sure that the temperature in the car never goes above 80.6°F (27°C); otherwise, the animal can suffer heat shock.

Vacation foster care: Perhaps you know of an acquaintance or relative who would take your hamster while you are away. He or she should, though, be able to build a relationship with small animals or perhaps even have some of his or her own.

In-house vacation substitute: Naturally you can also leave your hamster home and ask an acquaintance or a relative to look in on it every two or three days (see Animal-Sitter Checklist, page 136).

Small animal pet-boarding facilities: You read right, there are actually small animal hotels. Here, for a price, your hamster will be expertly cared for. You will find addresses on the Internet, in

(see page 53)

> ### TIP
>
> **Not cuddly animals**
>
> Point out to your visitors that hamsters are not cuddly animals and do not like to be handled by strangers. You will prevent the hamster from being stressed unnecessarily, and you will reduce the risk of becoming liable if the visitors are bitten.

◀ *Outsmart the hamster? How do you get it to go back into the cage? The food trail leads straight inside.*

specialized magazines, or in the classified ads in the newspapers.

One day before your departure, undertake a general cleaning of the cage and add fresh litter. If you are away for less than four weeks, the substitute caretaker should not be required to do such a cage cleaning.

Note: There is also the possibility of putting the hamster in an animal shelter, which I would advise against. Not that it would suffer improper care, but animal shelters house abandoned animals and most are so full, if not overburdened, that they cannot offer vacation care. But check with your local animal shelter to see what they offer.

What Do You Do If You Get Sick?

It is feasible to ask if the hamster can be infected when the owner is sick—for example, if you have the flu, is it advisable to avoid contact with your pet? As a rule that is not necessary. There are hardly any human diseases that can be transmitted to your hamster. Therefore, if you are not bedridden, you can continue to care for it without any concern. Only if you are physically unable should you ask someone to take over feeding the hamster. Also, if you find out after keeping a hamster for some time that you or another family member are allergic to hamster fur, another person must take over the care of the animal. In this case, it may even become necessary for you to be separated from the hamster altogether.

The Hamster Grows Old

Hamsters unfortunately have a short life, and it almost always ends too early for its human caretaker. So how can you tell if the hamster is getting old or is possibly sick? It is difficult if you do not know the birth date of your animal, for it is next to impossible to determine the age of an adult hamster. However, there are a few signs of aging changes:

The hamster no longer comes out of its sleeping house in the evening at the usual time but only much later.

It moves very slowly and deliberately.

It takes no more interest in exploring everything during free runs.

It goes onto the exercise wheel less often.

It eats and hoards only a little.

Its fur becomes disheveled.

The hamster loses fur (usually beginning in the head region).

The hamster has scabby places on its skin.

Its eyes become dull.

Its spine becomes bent.

The hamster loses weight.

If you confirm one or several of these signs in your hamster and have already been caring for it a long time, it could be that the sunset of its life is drawing closer. But if you are uncertain, you should immediately have the veterinarian examine your pet, since some of the symptoms listed can also indicate an illness.

Care of the old hamster: If you know for sure that your hamster is exhibiting signs of age, simply keep on caring for it as you have before. You need not change your habits. If the hamster is eating less, it also makes no sense to force it to eat more. On the other hand, you don't need to worry about a balanced diet anymore. If the hamster has favorite treats that it likes to eat, you can feel comfortable about giving it that pleasure more often. The hamster also no longer needs so much free running now. It will certainly have less and less interest in exploring anything new. On the contrary, try even harder to reduce the stress for your animal by letting it

have its rest and also not picking it up as often.

When the hamster dies: Although no one knows exactly, it is assumed that the animal does not suffer as a rule. One day the hamster will be lying rolled

Fellow Hamsters Mean Stress

▶ 1 **Hamsters** are loners. The confrontation with fellow hamsters causes the animals great stress and is always connected with aggressive disputes.

▶ 2 **In the cage,** the animals cannot avoid each other. This leads to fierce fights, which not infrequently lead to the death of one of the two participants.

Fun with hamster photography

Do you have a camera? If yes, then you can use it to document your hamster's various patterns of behavior. You will see how much fun it can be.

What to do:

Try to "catch" him in as many different situations as possible. Next, arrange the pictures according to the behavior traits described in the chapter The Typical Hamster. Does your hamster have characteristics that are not described there? Then the photos may be worth publishing on the Internet. On page 141 in the Addresses and Literature section, you will find addresses where you can exchange with other hamster-lovers in Internet forums.

Enter your observations here:

up and lifeless in its sleep house. Then it has fallen asleep peacefully. But some hamsters become ill in their old age because their immune systems are no longer functioning. They develop tumors or have problems with their digestive systems. Consult with your veterinarian. If he or she recommends that you have the animal put to sleep, you should follow this advice. To free the hamster of pain shortly before the end of its life is then the best you can still do for your pet. Together with your children, bury your pet in your garden or in a lovely spot. Moreover, you need have no concerns about burying the hamster in the garden. The burying of small animals in one's own property is legally permitted. You should maintain a minimum depth of 20 in. (50 cm). As to the children, especially those for whom the loss of a beloved animal can become a great emotional stress: you as parents should try as gently as possible to help the child over his or her grief (see page 88).

When the hamster is obviously ▶
healthy and content, you can be
proud of your good care.

Animal-Sitter Checklist

Do you want to go on vacation and have an animal sitter take care of your pet? You can write down everything your vacation substitute should know. This way your hamster will be optimally cared-for, and you can enjoy your vacation without a second thought!

My hamster is named:

My hamster looks like this:

My hamster likes to eat:

This much daily:

This much once a week:

Treats for between meals:

My hamster drinks this:

The proper feeding times:

The feed is stored here:

Housecleaning:

This gets cleaned daily:

This gets cleaned weekly:

My hamster loves these treats:

How you can keep it incredibly busy:

My hamster doesn't like this at all:

What my hamster is not allowed:

This is important as well:

This is my hamster's veterinarian:

My vacation address and telephone:

INDEX

Page numbers in **boldface** indicate illustrations.

V

W

Y

Z

ADDRESSES/ LITERATURE

Internet Hamster Association of North America
http://groups.msn.com /InternetHamsterAssoc

Calls itself: "A networking and resource site for hamster enthusiasts."

Hamster Club of Ontario
http://www.geocities.com/ hamsterclubofontario/home. html

The website says: "Membership in the HCO is a great way to become more involved in the hobby. We invite all hamster owners, breeders and exhibitors from our own province and beyond to join us."

Members can receive a newsletter four times per year, attend meetings, participate in hamster shows, obtain informational pamphlets, and meet other hamster owners.

California Hamster Association
http://www.geocities.com/ CalHamAssoc/

This is a nonprofit hamster club in Southern California that is interested in educating hamster owners, and improving the quality of hamsters in California and North America. It also arranges competitive hamster shows.

The National Hamster Council
http://www.hamsters-uk.org

The National Hamster Council is the oldest hamster club in the world. Although it is British, many North American hamster owners join one of its affiliated clubs because there are not many clubs in North America. Information about shows and breed standards is provided.

Popular Hamster Websites

www.petwebsite.com/ hamsters.asp
www.ahc.umn.edu/rar/MNA ALAS/Hamsters.html
http://exoticpets.about.com/ cs/hamsters/a/hamstercare. htm
http://www.hamsterific.com/ SyrianHamsters.cfm
http://www.ask-the-vet.com/ hamster-care.htm
http://www.hamsterhideout. com/allabthams.html
http://www.myhammie.com
http://www.hookedon hamsters.com
http://www.hamster-heaven.com/index.html
http://www.hamsterific.com/ DwarfHamsters.cfm
http://russiandwarfhamsters. tripod.com/hams/id1.html

BOOKS

Von Frisch, Otto. *Hamsters: A Complete Pet Owner's Manual.* Barron's Educational Series, Inc.

Hill, Lorraine. *Hamsters A to Z.* TFH Publications.

Bartlett, Patricia. *The Hamster Handbook.* Barron's Educational Series, Inc.

Bucsis, Gerry, and Sommerville, Barbara. *Training Your Pet Hamster.* Barron's Educational Series, Inc.

MAGAZINES

Critters USA magazine is an annual publication that has information about hamsters in every yearly issue.

THE PHOTOGRAPHS

The illustrations on the front and back covers, as well as the insides, show:
Front cover: golden hamster. Outer front flap (Test): top, golden hamster; bottom, Djungarian dwarf hamster. Inside front flap (Welcome): left-hand page: top right, satin hamster, circle, golden hamster, bottom left, golden hamster; right-hand page: top left, golden hamster female carrying a young animal, circle, golden hamster

coming out of clay house, bottom left, Campbell's short-tailed hamster, bottom right, long-haired hamster. Back cover: golden hamster. Outer back flap: the author, Peter Fritzsche. Inside back flap (from left to right): Djungarian dwarf hamster, satin hamster, golden hamster at his dish, Campbell's short-tailed hamster eating a piece of carrot.
Page 6: As happy as can be, the golden hamster explores his immediate surroundings.
Page 30: This Chinese hamster has made itself comfortable in the hollowed out coconut shell.
Page 48: The golden hamster is already quite tame. But watch out! A fall off the table could have fatal consequences.
Page 62: A millet spike is a healthy treat for golden hamsters.
Page 76: The Djungarian dwarf hamster explores the sunflower.
Page 94: This satin hamster feels cozy and snug in the sisal ball.
Page 108: Campbell's short-tailed hamster and baby.
Page 122: Long-haired golden hamster (light gray) on his first free run.

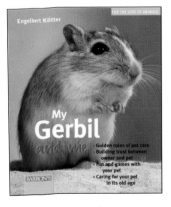
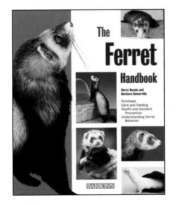

The Author

Dr. Peter Fritzsche is a scientific researcher at the Institute of Zoology of the Martin Luther University at Halle-Wittenberg, from which he also received his doctorate. For the last 30 years, he has dedicated himself to research in the behavioral biology of hamsters. Through countless lectures and publications in professional journals, Peter Fritzsche has become recognized throughout Europe as an expert in all questions about hamsters' habits. Personally he has been interested in various pets since he was ten years old, chief among them all, hamsters.

The Photographer

Oliver Giel specializes in nature and animal photography. His pictures are published in many magazines and animal-care books. All photographs are by Oliver Giel, with the exception of: Dr. Peter Fritzsche: pages 8, left and right, 9, and 50, left; Regina Kuhn: pages 24, left, 25, right top and bottom, 26, top left and right.

First edition for the United States, its territories and dependencies and Canada published in 2008 by Barron's Educational Series, Inc.

Published originally under the title *mein Hamster*, in the series *mein Heimtier*
© 2006 Gräfe und Unzer Verlag GmbH, München

GU

English translation © copyright 2008 by Barron's Educational Series, Inc.
Translation from German by Elizabeth D. Crawford

All inquiries should be addressed to:
Barron's Educational Series, Inc.
250 Wireless Boulevard
Hauppauge, NY 11788
www.barronseduc.com

ISBN-13: 0-978-7641-3713-6
ISBN-10: 0-7641-3713-1

Library of Congress Cataloging-in-Publication Data

Fritzsche, Peter.
    [Mein Hamster. English]
    My hamster / Peter Fritzsche ; translation from the German by Elizabeth D. Crawford.
        p. cm. — (My pet)
    ISBN-13: 978-0-7641-3713-6 (alk. paper)
    ISBN-10: 0-7641-3713-1 (alk. paper)
1. Hamsters as pets.   I. Title.

    SF459.H3F7513 2007
    636.935'6—dc22

                                                2007018592

Printed and bound in China

9 8 7 6 5 4 3 2

Thanks

I, Peter Fritzsche, thank my daughter Karoline for the contribution of her years of experience with small animal keeping and of collaboration on this guide. I thank the working group on behavioral biology at the Institute of Zoology Halle, under the direction of Prof. Rolf Gattermann for the many new findings in the biology of the hamster discovered in our work together. I am forever grateful to the publisher and his editors for the good teamwork throughout this project.